*A Guide for Beginners*

# Understanding the Gospels

Anthony J. Marinelli

**Paulist Press** New York/Mahwah, N.J.

*also by Anthony J. Marinelli*
*published by Paulist Press*

YAHWEH AND SON:
  A TEENAGER'S GUIDE TO THE BIBLE

Acknowledgments
Scripture selections taken from the *New American Bible,* copyright © 1970 by the Confraternity of Christian Doctrine, Washington, D.C., are used with permission. All rights reserved.

Copyright © 1988
by Anthony J. Marinelli

All rights reserved. No part of this book may be reproduced or transmitted in any form or by any means, electronic or mechanical, including photocopying, recording or by any information storage and retrieval system without permission in writing from the Publisher.

Library of Congress Cataloging-in-Publication Data

Marinelli, Anthony J.
    Understanding the Gospels.

    1. Bible. N.T. Gospels—Criticism, interpretation, etc. I. Title.
BS2555.2.M335    1989    226'.061    88-25388
ISBN 0-8091-3037-8 (pbk.)

Published by Paulist Press
997 Macarthur Blvd.
Mahwah, N.J. 07430

Printed and bound in the United States of America

# Contents

Introduction 1

Formation of the Gospels 3

The New Testament World 15

The Coming of the Reign of God 33

The Synoptic Gospels 54

The Gospel of John 73

The Death and Resurrection of Jesus 94

Suggested Reading for Further Study 110

DEDICATED TO MY FRIENDS,
COLLEAGUES AND STUDENTS
AT HOLY TRINITY HIGH SCHOOL

# Introduction

It is sometimes said that we live in a "post-Christian" age in which the findings of modern science and the insights of contemporary psychology have made religious faith obsolete. Yet we continue to ask religious questions: What is the meaning of our lives? Is there a meaning and destination to the world? Does it really ultimately matter how we live our lives? The answers given by the church have been challenged and rejected by some. Is it possible that a carpenter/preacher from Palestine who lived nearly two thousand years ago can help reveal to us the meaning of our own humanity? Is it possible that through this man God has spoken his word to his children? Is it possible for an intelligent, creative, and contemporary human being to follow Jesus Christ? The only place to really begin to answer these questions is in the four gospels contained in the New Testament. They are certainly not the only place to look, but they are the inescapable beginning.

This book is written for those interested in such a beginning. It is the work not of a Scripture scholar but of an educator. It is an attempt to clarify for the reader the findings of Scripture scholarship without the complexity and the technical language of the scholars. This book will run the risk of oversimplifying complex issues, but at the same time it will offer the advantage of looking at the whole without being swallowed by the parts.

I have tried to take little or nothing for granted in explaining how to read and understand the gospels. I have also tried to include as many scriptural examples in the text as possible. My experience tells me that listing the reference means that it rarely gets read. The main thrust of my approach is to try to uncover the inspired meaning of the gospel passages. What was the message that Matthew, Mark, Luke, and John wanted to communicate to their audiences and how can that message serve as "inspiration" for believers today?

The measure of success for this book is whether or not it leads the reader away from it and into the gospels themselves. Reading a book *about* the gospels is a pale substitute for reading the gospels themselves. This book is written with the conviction that the message, life, death and resurrection of Jesus Christ offers human beings both the personal and the communal fulfillment that they seek. However, that life and message did not exist in a vacuum. It is the purpose of this book to shed light on the factors that influenced both Jesus and those who recorded the gospels for future posterity.

There are two people that I would like to thank for their role in this book. The first is my editor at Paulist Press, Doug Fisher, who has always offered great encouragement on this and other writing assignments. The second is my wife, Pat, for contributions too numerous to mention.

# 1

# Formation of the Gospels

## The Gospel: The Good News of Jesus Christ

The word "gospel" has several different uses. It is one of the readings at Mass. It is also a book in the Bible (in fact, four books: Matthew, Mark, Luke and John). But its original meaning is neither of these. The gospel was originally the good news proclaimed by Jesus Christ. Mark summarizes the teaching of Jesus with this proclamation: "This is the time of fulfillment. The reign of God is at hand. Reform your lives and believe in the gospel" (Mark 1:15). The word we find in the New Testament is "euaggelion" which meant a proclamation of good news. We really cannot understand the four gospels unless we understand this original sense. Christian faith is based on the good news of Jesus who offered God's unconditional love and mercy to the people of his time and ultimately to the world.

### The Oral Gospel

After the death and resurrection of Jesus, the good news that Jesus proclaimed became the good news about Jesus himself. The early church believed that Jesus was the fulfillment of God's promises and that through him God had offered salvation to the world. This basic proclamation of faith, called the kerygma, was accompanied by stories about Jesus and his message. These stories were passed from one community to the next and from one generation to the next. This "oral tradition" became the second phase of the gospel.

### *The Written Word*

Finally, the gospels reached their written form when the evangelists (gospel authors) compiled their narratives based on various sources within the Christian community. It is generally accepted among scholars that Mark was the first of the evangelists, writing his gospel approximately in the year 70 A.D.

Thus, the written gospels as we now know them went through three stages of development:

1. the teaching and preaching of Jesus (ca. 30 A.D.–33 A.D.)
2. the oral gospel in the early church (ca. 33 A.D.–70 A.D.)
3. the written gospels (ca. 70 A.D.–100 A.D.)

### *The Gospels: Documents of Faith*

The most common error that people make when reading the gospels is to think that they are biographies of Jesus. They are not. The gospels were originally written as teaching tools within the early church meant to evoke and deepen faith in Christ. Unlike a biography, the gospels were not interested in objectivity and precise accuracy of details. To the contrary, they were more interested in communicating the meaning of Jesus' life as Lord and Savior than in the specific details of that life. As we can see from the information above, the gospels are not eyewitness reports of the events. Their purpose is to instruct, inspire and give testimony to faith in Jesus.

## Jesus of History and the Christ of Faith

Throughout the ministry of Jesus, the people and even his own disciples had very little understanding of who Jesus was. It was only at the resurrection that the disciples recognized what he meant to the history and salvation of the world. The encounter with the risen Lord was different than meeting the earthly Jesus. The revelation of Jesus as risen meant more than his life continuing beyond death. It revealed Jesus as the universal Lord and Messiah. Those who met the risen Lord had their own lives transformed in the process.

When the evangelists compiled the gospels, they did so with a knowledge that was unavailable to anyone during the earthly life of Jesus. The gospels, as such, are **post-resurrectional documents.** The evangelists wrote about Jesus of Nazareth from the perspective of the resurrection and faith in the risen Lord. They not only wrote about the words and deeds of Jesus but included an interpretation of those words and deeds. Thus, the gospels give us not only the **Jesus of history** but the **Christ of faith** as well.

## The Tools of Interpretation

In order to understand the gospels, it is necessary to study the documents in light of the various influences upon them. Rather than threatening the truth of God's word, this process will enable us to have a deeper insight into that truth. In order to help us uncover the meaning of the gospels, we will look at four different methods (or "criticisms") employed by Scripture scholars.

A careful reading of Matthew, Mark and Luke will reveal a tremendous amount of similarity among the three. For this reason, they are known as the synoptic gospels, meaning from the same point of view. Almost ninety percent of Mark's gospel can also be found in Matthew and about half of it in

Luke. There is also material in Matthew and in Luke that is virtually identical yet is not in Mark. These facts provoke the scholars to ask what sources were used by these evangelists. Who copied from whom and how do these sources affect the meanings of the gospels? The problem with discovering the sources of these three gospels is commonly referred to as the "synoptic problem."

There are several theories on the solution to the synoptic problem, but here we will present only the one that enjoys a very widespread acceptance among scholars today. The solution is, of course, only an hypothesis, but seems to be the one that best describes the available facts.

Most scholars today believe that Mark's gospel was the first to be written, approximately forty years after the death of Jesus or ca. 70 A.D. Matthew and Luke wrote their gospels independently of one another about fifteen years after Mark. Both Matthew and Luke had Mark's gospel available to them and at times took passages from it verbatim and at other times enhanced the text with their own style and to suit their own purposes. What is confusing is the identical material in Matthew and Luke that is not in Mark. Where did this come from? It could not have been passed down so precisely within an oral tradition. For this reason, it is believed that Matthew and Luke had another written document available to them that was lost in the early days of the church. This source which is made up mostly of sayings and teachings of Jesus, is commonly known as the Q document (from the German word "Quelle" meaning "source"). Of course, in addition to the material from Mark and Q, Matthew and Luke also have a great deal of material unique to their own gospels.

Even a quick look at John's gospel will reveal that it is unique among the four. This gospel was the last to be written (90–110 A.D.) and takes a very different approach to the person and message of Jesus. John was probably aware of the other three gospels, but he does not use them as direct sources. Instead, the author seems to rely on a unique oral tradition and theology. We will say much more about this later. In summary, this diagram describes the various sources used by the evangelists:

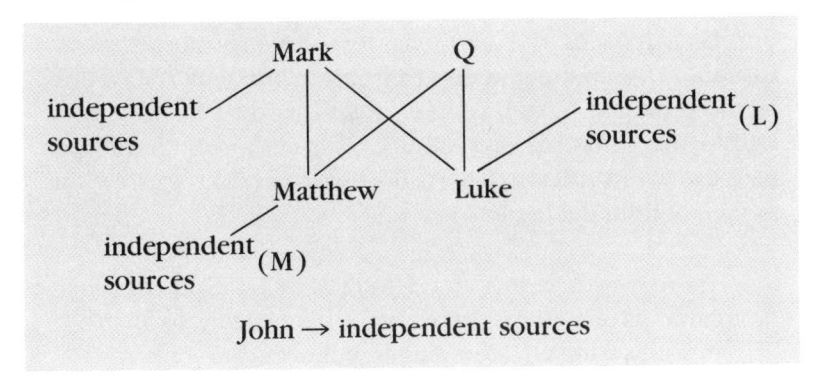

```
                    Mark         Q
  independent         \   \   /   /  independent
  sources              \   \ /   /   sources      (L)
                        \   X   /
                         \ / \ /
                          X   X
                         / \ / \
                    Matthew   Luke
       independent
       sources  (M)

            John → independent sources
```

*Form Criticism*

Source criticism helped the scholars understand where the written word came from, but it didn't tell them a great deal about how that word had come to be shaped by the oral tradition. This was to be the role of form criticism. The form critics tried to analyze the various stages of development involved in the formation of the gospels. The underlying assumption of form criticism is that the stories in the gospels have been shaped by their authors to fit the specific needs and situations of their communities. These situations (commonly referred to by the German "sitz im leben") refer generally to two different levels of the gospel: first, the situation in the life of Jesus, and, second, the situation in the life of the church. The form critics are more concerned with the second level.

The various elements within the gospels can be categorized according to how they first appeared as spoken elements within the faith community. For example, within the gospel we can distinguish among narratives, testimonies, hymns, prayers, sayings, parables and mythic stories. The form critic attempts to appraise the various parts of the gospel in order to better understand their origin and later use by the evangelist.

Let's look at the first chapter of John's gospel as an example. The first eighteen verses are commonly referred to as the prologue. This prologue was formerly a hymn known within the Christian community. The author of the gospel uses the hymn and also inserts his own material regarding the person of John the Baptist:

> There was a man named John sent by God, who came as a witness to testify to the light, so that through him all men might believe—but only to testify to the light, for he himself was not the light. The real light which gives light to every man was coming into the world (John 1:6–9).

The form critic can help us see that the original hymn is diverted to a section of teaching about the role of the Baptist. The verses above emphasize the fact that the Baptist is not the Christ. It seems that there existed some groups who were still followers of John the Baptist late in the first century. This passage in John is responding to that "sitz im leben." He emphasizes that these people have misunderstood the true role of the Baptist.

*Redaction Criticism*

As you can probably tell by now, the evangelists were in some ways more like editors than authors, compiling and adapting material from various sources. However, each of the gospel writers also brought to his work a unique theological insight into the person of Jesus. They were able to use the various elements in the gospel to suit their own purposes. This aspect of the gospels is known as redaction or editing. Redaction criticism seeks to discover the influence of the author upon the written work. The four gospels give us portraits of Jesus but with the unique genius of each artist. Redaction criticism seeks to discover how the gospel reflects not only the words and deeds of Jesus but the theological interests of the author as well. We will examine this in greater depth later in the book, but now let's take a look at the basic themes of each of the gospel writers.

**Mark.** Scripture scholars are uncertain who the author of Mark's gospel was. Some believe it to be a man named John Mark who is mentioned in the Acts of the Apostles as a missionary companion of St. Paul. However, there is no consensus on this. Whoever the author was, he was writing to a Christian community that was suffering persecution, very possibly the community in Rome that was feeling the wrath of the Roman emperor. Because of this, Mark emphasizes that Jesus is not a Messiah who comes in power and glory, but is a humble servant willing to take on suffering as the price of fidelity to God's will. At the heart of Mark's gospel is the message to his people not to lose heart in the face of persecution but to find hope in the fact that their Savior also suffered. Those who follow Jesus must be willing to follow the way of the cross.

Also at the core of Mark's theology is the "messianic secret," Jesus' refusal to declare himself the Messiah, and the bewilderment of the people who encounter Jesus as they try to understand who he is.

**Matthew.** Most Christians who read the gospels and hear them read at Mass on Sunday assume that the author of this gospel was the apostle Matthew. This, however, is almost impossible. It was probably written in the 80's, by which time all the apostles had died. The author of this gospel was a well-educated Jew, possibly a scribe, who was writing to an audience made up largely of Jewish Christians—Christians who had been born and raised in the faith of Israel, as opposed to Gentile Christians who were originally members of pagan religions or no religion at all. Matthew's overriding concern is to show that Jesus is the fulfillment of Judaism, the faith of Israel. He is the one that all the prophecies pointed to in a hidden way, and he brings salvation to Israel and the whole world. He is the new Moses and fulfills the law given on Mount Sinai (the ten commandments) with the law of love.

**Luke.** The theological themes of Luke's gospel are not as immediately apparent as those of Matthew and Mark. The gospel of Luke is the first part of a two part work which concludes with the Acts of the Apostles. In these two volumes Luke traces the development of Christianity from its humble origins in Bethlehem to its establishment in the heart of the Gentile world, in the city of Rome. Luke's concern is to show that there are no limits on the good news of salvation. Jesus is the Savior of all mankind, and in a special way he comes to the poor, the oppressed and the outcast.

In order to make this point more concrete, let's look at Luke and Matthew's portrayal of the birth of Jesus, keeping in mind what we have said about the themes of their gospels. Read Matthew 1–2 and Luke 1–3.

## Matthew: Jesus, the fulfillment of the faith of Israel
1. Traces the genealogy of Jesus back to Abraham, the father of Jewish faith.
2. Quotes from the Hebrew Scriptures five times to show Jesus as the fulfillment of the passages.
3. The personality of Joseph is built on Old Testament characters and he is the hero of the story.

4. Jesus, like Moses, must escape an attempt on his life as an infant and flees to a foreign land.

## Luke: Jesus, the Savior of all people
1. Traces the genealogy of Jesus back to Adam, the father of all mankind.
2. Mary is the heroine of the story because of her humble openness to the will of God.
3. Jesus is born in humble origins, a stable in Bethlehem with shepherds as his guests.

As you can see, Matthew and Luke tell the story of Jesus' birth in very different ways, emphasizing the main themes of their gospel as they relate the narrative.

**John.** The fourth gospel is unique in its portrayal of Jesus and his message. The gospel was not written by the apostle John, but may have been written by his disciples. This gospel wished to make very clear that Jesus is the Son of God from all eternity. At the heart of this work is the theology of the incarnation, the belief that God has become a human being. More than any of the synoptics, John's gospel comes across as a post-resurrectional interpretation of the person of Jesus. Although it certainly contains many historically accurate details about the ministry of Jesus, much of John's gospel also represents his editorial reworking of the deeds and words of Jesus.

*Historical Criticism*

The term historical criticism is most often used to describe the entire process of scientific biblical studies, but here we are using it in a more limited sense. Historical criticism refers to the study of the people, traditions, religious ideas, culture and politics of the New Testament era. Ironically, we have, in the twentieth century, a better grasp of the history of the New Testament era than did the people living in the second century. Thanks in large part to developments in archaeology, technology and communication, we have greater access to the thought forms and traditions that shaped the gospels than did the people reading them for the next nineteen hundred years. The next chapter will be devoted to a look at the New Testament world, so here we use only one example of how historical criticism helps to enlighten our understanding of the New Testament.

Throughout history, some Christians have unfortunately tried to use the gospels as the basis of a thoroughly un-Christian attitude—antisemitism. Historical criticism helps unmask this prejudice by revealing the thoroughly Jewish character of Jesus' spirituality and personality. Jesus himself was nurtured in the faith of Israel, especially its prophets. Likewise, historical criticism has helped reveal the probability that the Roman government had an equally important hand in the death of Christ.

### Excerpt from "Instruction on the Historical Truth of the Gospels," Pontifical Biblical Commission, April 21, 1964

*... In order to bring out with fullest clarity the enduring truth and authority of the gospels he (the Scripture scholar) must ... make skillful use of the new aids to exegesis, especially those which the historical method, taken in its widest sense, has provided....*

*... it need not be denied that the apostles, when handing on to their hearers the things which in actual fact the Lord had said and done, did so in light of that fuller understanding which they enjoyed as result of being schooled by the glori-*

> *ous things accomplished in Christ, and of being illumined by the Spirit of Truth. Thus, it came about that just as Jesus himself after his resurrection had "interpreted to them" both the words of the Old Testament and the words which he himself had spoken, so now they in their turn interpreted his words and deeds according to the needs of their hearers.... The sacred authors selected certain things out of the many which had been handed on; some they synthesized, some they explained with an eye to the situation of the churches, painstakingly using every means of bringing home to their readers the solid truth of the things in which they had been instructed.*

## Summary

1. The gospels are the product of the early Christian community, and can best be understood in light of the world in which they were written and the people for whom they were written.
2. The gospels are not biographies of Jesus but testimonials of faith based on historical remembrances of Jesus and the "oral tradition" of those stories.
3. The synoptic gospels (Mark, Matthew and Luke) share a great deal of common material, with Mark serving as the basis for the other two.
4. The gospels are post-resurrectional documents written in light of the church's faith in the risen Jesus.
5. Scripture scholars make use of various methods of interpretation to help rediscover the original meaning of the gospels.
6. Source criticism analyzes the various sources used by the evangelists.
7. Form criticism studies the original "forms" that the mate-

rial in the gospels had taken as narratives, sayings, hymns, miracle stories, etc.
8. Redaction criticism attempts to discover the influence of the author's theology and interests on the written document.
9. Historical criticism seeks to locate the gospels within the social, religious, political and cultural situations of that era.

## Study Questions

1. What are the three layers of development in the formation of the written gospels?

2. How is a gospel different from a biography?

3. What is meant by the statement: "The gospels are post-resurrectional documents"? What is its significance in interpreting the gospels?

4. What is the difference between the Jesus of history and the Christ of faith?

5. What is the synoptic problem and how do scholars seek to answer it?

6. Define source, form, redaction and historical criticism.

7. Compare the stories of the call of the first disciples in each of the gospels: Matthew 4:18–22; Mark 1:14–20; Luke 5:1–11; John 1:35–50.

(a) In light of what you know about source criticism, why are Matthew and Mark's so similar? Why is John's so different?

(b) In light of what you know about redaction criticism, why do you think Luke and John reshaped the stories the way that they did?

# 2

# The New Testament World

**Christian faith has always affirmed an essential belief concerning Jesus: he was truly God, and he was truly human.** In fact, however, Christians throughout the centuries have always found the divinity of Jesus easier to accept than the humanity. It is not uncommon for Christians to profess belief in the humanity of Jesus while they really believe that he only looked human, but inside he was really God. The church has consistently rejected this interpretation. Jesus really was human. He shared the fullness of our humanity. If this is so, then **in order to understand the person of Christ we must understand the time and place in which he lived.** No human being ever exists in a vacuum. Our self-understanding always and only takes place within the context of a certain culture and society. Even if we reject many of the values of our culture, we are never isolated entities. Jesus, if he was truly a human being, also knew himself in the context of the time and circumstances in which he was born and raised. In this chapter, we would like to look at the religious, political and social structures that existed at the time of Christ and in the early church. We must become associated with the world of Palestine nearly two thousand years ago if we are to understand the gospel and the person of Jesus Christ.

*The Political Situation*

At the time of Jesus' birth, Palestine was a part of the great Roman Empire. The people of Israel had been through a period of near continual domination by foreign countries for the better part of the past six centuries. In 586 B.C. the kingdom of Judah was defeated by Babylonia and many of the people taken from their land into exile. Although they would eventually return to Palestine, the Jewish people would continue to be dominated by the Persians, the Greeks and finally the Romans in the year 63 B.C. **For the people of Israel, occupation of the land by foreigners was the cruelest of fates.** Their land had more than emotional and nationalistic meaning to them: **it was the land promised by their God, Yahweh.** It was the promise made to their forefather, Abraham: a sign of the fact that they were God's chosen people.

Originally, the Roman control of Israel was a benevolent one. They allowed **Herod the Great,** a Jew, to rule with full authority as king of the region. It was under the reign of Herod that Jesus was born. According to Matthew's gospel, Herod tried to have Jesus killed as an infant in order to protect his own power. While there is no other historical account of Herod's massacre of the innocents of Bethlehem, it certainly would have been in keeping with what we do know about him. According to historians of the era, Herod the Great was a bonafide pathological personality, insanely jealous of losing any of his power to the point of killing several members of his own family including two of his own sons.

Herod was succeeded in 4 B.C. by his three sons, **Archelaus, Herod Antipas and Philip.** Archelaus was given the major portion of land including Samaria, Idumea and Judea. Herod Antipas ruled over the area of Galilee and Perea, while Philip had the lands to the north and east of the sea of Galilee.

Very little is mentioned of Philip in the New Testament. However, he was the most successful and capable leader of the three. Herod Antipas was a shrewd calculating leader (Jesus calls him "that fox" in Luke 13:32) who married his half-brother's sister, Salome. This was a violation of the Mosaic law and brought with it the condemnation of John the Baptist who was eventually killed by Herod for his opposition to the marriage. Archelaus proved to be as unpopular as his father. He served for nine years before finally being removed by the Roman authorities at the constant behest of the people. The region that he ruled was then made a Roman province and ruled by a procurator, the most famous of which was **Pontius Pilate** (23–36 A.D.) who ruled the area with an iron hand and was very unpopular with the people of the region. While the gospels tend to portray Pilate as a stooge of the Jewish authorities, his torture and execution of Jesus would have been consistent with his violent and anti-Semitic personality. The tendency of the gospels to place the blame for Jesus' death exclusively with the Jews probably reflects the later animosity between Jewish and Christian groups in the latter part of the first century A.D.

*Messianic Expectations*

Why is it that so many of the Jewish people failed to recognize Jesus as the Messiah? Many Christians like to tell themselves that if they lived at the time of Christ, they certainly would have been one of his followers. However, the chances are great that they too would have missed the coming of the messiah because Jesus was not what people were expecting. Today the word messiah has the general meaning of someone who saves his people, but for the Jews there was a long historical background to the meaning of the messiah.
**The Hebrew word "masiah" (messiah) is the equiva-**

**lent of the Greek word "Christos" (Christ) and literally means "the anointed one."** Thus the name Jesus Christ is not really a name at all but a profession of faith meaning that Jesus is the Messiah. As a title, the term messiah originally referred to the Jewish king as the anointed or chosen of God. Beginning with **King David** (approximately 1000 B.C.) the Jewish people began to see their relationship with God (the covenant) connected closely to the idea of the king as God's anointed, the living sign of the covenant. We see this idea of the covenant in the second book of Samuel in the prophecy of Nathan to David: "Your house and your kingdom shall endure forever before me; your throne shall stand firm forever" (2 Samuel 7:16). The notion of the messiah originally had little to do with a salvific figure. Unfortunately, however, the Jewish kings were rarely good signs of that relationship. Before too long, the people of Israel began to look for the day when God would send a true messiah unlike the corrupt kings who ruled them. The notion of the messiah began to take on new meanings. It was now often associated with a figure who would restore Israel to its true identity as God's people. Following the **exile** (586–537 B.C.), the notion of messiah often became associated with the establishment of the reign of God: the day on which the lion and the lamb would lie down together, when the law of Israel would be observed from the heart, when God would relieve Israel from its suffering and oppression.

### *Jesus: A Different Messiah*

At the time of Jesus the notion of messiah was a combination of ideas varying somewhat from one group of Jews to the next. The dominant expectations, however, included the idea that the messiah would be descended from David, restore Israel to prominence and bring about the day of Yahweh (the kingdom of God). For most, this meant the re-establishment of Israel as a great nation: God's people in their own land observing the **Torah**. Some saw this deliverance as a great **apocalyptic event:** God dramatically and decisively reversing the lot of his people and creating a world filled with peace (shalom), judging the wicked and restoring the righteous. John the Baptist seemed to have this idea. In chastising the Pharisees for their lack of sincerity, he describes the coming of the messiah after him: "Who told you to flee from the wrath that is to come? . . . I baptize with water for the sake of reform, but the one who will follow me is more powerful than I. . . . His winnowing fan is in his hand. He will clear the threshing floor and gather his grain into his barn, but the chaff he will burn in unquenchable fire" (Matthew 3:7,11a,12). John's description of the coming messiah is one that is based on the notion of divine judgment and power. It is not surprising then that the Baptist is later confused by the words and deeds of Jesus who announces not God's judgment but his mercy and grace. Luke tells us that he sends two of his own disciples to ask Jesus if he is truly the messiah. Jesus gives them this response: "Go and report to John what you have seen and heard. The blind recover their sight, cripples walk, lepers are cured, the deaf hear, dead men are raised to life, and the poor have the good news preached to them. Blest is that man who finds no stumbling block in me" (Luke 7:22–23). Jesus' understanding of who the messiah is stands in conflict with the ideas of the people and even with the prophet who announced his coming.

### *Religious Traditions: The Temple and the Feasts*

It is very easy to become confused about first century Judaism from a twentieth century perspective. Today when we think of the temple, we usually think of the local synagogue, the place where our friends and neighbors go to worship and study. However, at the time of Jesus, and for centuries before him, there was only one temple and it was in the holy city of Jerusalem. The function of the temple was different than that of the local synagogue. The temple was the place where sacrifice was offered to God. Each day an unblemished lamb and incense would be offered as part of the cult surrounding the temple. Unlike the local **synagogues** which were led by the rabbis and Pharisees, only the priestly class could take part in temple service. The Jewish people would pay a temple tax and pilgrimage to the holy city on three feasts: **Passover, Pentecost and Tabernacles.** (Of course, not all Jews made the pilgrimage each year.)

The Passover was the central feast within the faith of Israel that recalled the exodus from Egypt and the saving power of God liberating his people from bondage. Each year the Jewish people would "relive" the exodus in the traditional seder meal. This feast was celebrated in the spring and followed fifty days later by the feast of Pentecost which originated as an agricultural feast and later celebrated the giving of the law to Moses on Mount Sinai. The feast of Tabernacles was celebrated in the fall originally as a thanksgiving for the harvest and later to recall the Jewish journey in the desert in search of the promised land.

As well as serving its ritual function, the temple had an equally important symbolic role. **It stood as a symbol of the faith of Israel and was the dwelling place of the one true God.** This all-important notion of the centrality of God and his unity with his people was also expressed in the great prayer and commandment, the *Shema Israel:*

> Hear O Israel! The Lord is our God, the Lord alone! Therefore you shall love the Lord, your God, with all your heart, and with all your soul, and with all your strength.

*The Torah*

For most people, the heart and soul of their faith was lived in the daily observance of the law or the Torah. The law was much more than a group of religious rules and regulations. **The law was the lifeblood of the covenant** with Yahweh. It was the path to righteousness, the way of life. The author of Psalm 1 describes it thus:

> Happy the man who follows not the counsel of the wicked
> nor walks in the way of sinners
> nor sits in the company of the insolent,
> but delights in the law of the Lord
> and meditates on his law day and night.
> He is like a tree planted near running water,
> that yields its fruit in due season,
> and whose leaves never fade.
> (Whatever he does, prospers.)

## Israel: A People of Hope

The early church understood Jesus to be the fulfillment of the hopes of their forefathers. In him, the promises of God were made complete:

*to Abraham:* "I will make of you a great nation, and I will bless you; I will make your name great, so that you will be a blessing." (Genesis 12:2)

*to Jacob:* "I am God almighty; be fruitful and multiply.

> A nation, indeed an assembly of nations,
> shall stem from you,
> and kings shall issue from your loins."
> (Genesis 35:11)

*to Moses:* "You have seen for yourself how I have treated the Egyptians and how I bore you up on eagle wings and brought you here to myself. Therefore, if you hearken to my voice and keep my covenant, you shall be my special possession, dearer to me than all other people, though all the earth is mine. You shall be to me a kingdom of priests, a holy nation." (Exodus 19:4–6)

*to David:* "Your house and your kingdom shall endure forever before me; your throne shall stand firm forever." (2 Samuel 7:16)

*to Isaiah:* "But a shoot shall sprout from the stump of Jesse,
and from his roots a bud shall blossom.
The spirit of the Lord shall rest upon him:
a spirit of wisdom and understanding,
a spirit of counsel and of strength,
a spirit of knowledge and fear of the Lord,
and his delight shall be the fear of the Lord.
Not by appearance shall he judge,
nor by hearsay shall he decide.
But he will judge the poor with justice
and decide aright for the land's afflicted."

*to Jeremiah:* "The days are coming, says the Lord, when I will make a new covenant with the house of

Israel and the house of Judah. It will not be like the covenant I made with their fathers the day I took them by the hand to lead them forth from the land of Egypt; for they broke my covenant, and I had to show myself their master, says the Lord. But this is the covenant which I will make with the house of Israel after those days, says the Lord. I will place my law within them, and write it upon their hearts; I will be their God, and they shall be my people. No longer will they have need to teach their friends and relatives how to know the Lord. All, from least to greatest, shall know me, says the Lord, for I will forgive their evildoing and remember their sin no more."

## *The Cast of Characters*

The Jewish people who lived at the time of Christ were certainly not a monolithic group who all thought, acted and believed the same way. Similar to Christianity today, there was a variety of beliefs within Judaism varying from one group to the next. These groups are often mentioned in the gospels and we need to understand them if we are to understand the gospels.

## *Pharisees*

The group most often mentioned in the gospels are the Pharisees. These were Jewish laymen who believed in a strict interpretation of both the oral and written law. The law, or the **Torah** as it is known, is at the heart of all Jewish life and spirituality. The Pharisees, however, also insisted on adherence to the oral interpretations of the law by the scribes.

These oral interpretations were eventually codified and written in the documents known as the mishnah and the **Talmud.** The word **"Pharisee" means "separate one"** which refers to their habit of avoiding the masses of people less pious than they as well as the **Gentiles** (non-Jewish foreigners). The Pharisees served an extremely important role within Judaism. More than any other group they helped preserve Judaism through the first century A.D. because of their unwillingness to give in to the influences of the foreign cultures that occupied Palestine. **The gospels most often portray them at odds with Jesus over his ease in associating with sinners.** Jesus, on the other hand, is often seen taking them to task for a rigid legalism that puts the law above the needs of people. It is very possible that the picture that we get of the Pharisees in the gospels is somewhat exaggerated. It is very hard to find a single good word about them. This may reflect the situation of the church as much as it does the historical reality. There is no doubt that Jesus came into conflict with the Pharisees, but the nature and the depth of it have probably been expanded by the gospel authors.

*Sadducees*

**The Sadducees were an aristocratic and priestly class who wielded political as well as religious power.** They generally looked down at the Pharisees, perceiving them as a lay movement interfering with their priestly duties and privileges. The Sadducees exercised control of the temple and its worship. Unlike the Pharisees, the Sadducees accepted only the written Torah and no further additions. For this reason they did not accept the idea of life after death as the Pharisees did. (Jesus sided with the Pharisees in this debate as Matthew explains in 22:23–33.) In fact, they were rather indifferent to important religious issues and saw the oral interpretations as a further nuisance. The Sadducees were a wealthy class who exercised power in the Jewish council known as the **Sanhedrin**. **Caiaphas,** the high priest who presided over the trial against Jesus that eventually led to his death, was a Sadducee.

*Essenes*

Essenes are not specifically referred to in the gospels yet they were an important group during the time of Christ. These Jews left the traditional forms of temple worship to **live an ascetical life in the desert** following the writing of the prophets. **John the Baptist** may possibly have been an Essene or have been influenced by them. Recent archeological finds have uncovered important documents of the Essene community known as the **Dead Sea Scrolls.** These have provided invaluable insight into the world and the people of the New Testament.

*Scribes*

Another important group that often surfaces in the New Testament are the scribes who are very often associated with the Pharisees. Scribes were a part of most near eastern civilizations where reading and writing skills were reserved for the few. **In New Testament times the scribe was the one who was the expert in Jewish law.** Many of the scribes belonged to the party of the Pharisees and believed in strict interpretation of the law. Like the Pharisees, the scribes mentioned in the gospels are often in conflict with Jesus. They would have strongly objected to Jesus' teaching on his own authority, for they believed the law to be the source of all righteousness and learning.

### Zealots

Also within Judaism were **those who measured the coming of the messiah only in terms of national liberation and freedom from oppression.** These were known as zealots, and their primary purpose was to rid Palestine of its Roman influence. The zealot movement was relatively calm during the ministry of Jesus, although one of his apostles is called a zealot (Simon the zealot, not to be confused with Simon the fisherman, later called Simon Peter). The zealots used terrorist tactics and were generally hated by both Jews and Romans. They led a revolt against Rome in the late sixties that ultimately led to the destruction of the temple.

### Samaritans

Unlike Pharisees, Sadducees, Essenes and zealots, the name Samaritan has managed to survive as a regular part of English usage, almost always in conjunction with the adjective "good." A good Samaritan is a commonplace description of someone who goes out of one's way to help a stranger. This was hardly the meaning of Samaritan at the time of Jesus. A **Samaritan was the most despised of all persons by the Jews.** The origins of the antipathy between Jews and Samaritans is not completely clear but they were deeply rooted in history. These people lived in Samaria. They were worshipers of the God of Israel but held several foreign beliefs and worshiped at the temple on Mount Gerizim rather than in Jerusalem. They had intermarried with pagans and over the years the growing animosity between Jews and Samaritans placed them in lower esteem than even the Gentiles. This animosity is detected in the gospels when Jesus stopped to talk with a Samaritan woman (John 4:27). His apostles were shocked that he would do such a thing. (In fact, his actions were doubly surprising, because she was a woman as well as a

Samaritan.) And in the famous story of the good Samaritan in Luke's gospel, Jesus purposely chooses the despised Samaritan as the hero of the story to emphasize his point that love has no boundaries.

### *Tax Collectors*

Among the Jewish people themselves, no group was more thoroughly despised than the tax collectors. These were Jews who worked for the Romans (in itself a sacrilege) and were notorious for their dishonest ways. In the gospels, they often are included among those outcasts of society befriended by Jesus. In fact, one of Jesus' apostles was originally a tax collector.

> As he moved on he saw Levi, the son of Alphaeus at his tax collector's post, and said to him, "Follow me." Levi got up and became his follower. While Jesus was reclining to eat in Levi's house, many tax collectors and those known as sinners joined him and his disciples at dinner. The number of those who followed him was large. When the scribes who belonged to the Pharisee party saw that he was eating with tax collectors and sinners, they complained to his disciples, "Why does he eat with such as these?" Overhearing the remark, Jesus said to them, "People who are healthy do not need a doctor; sick people do. I have come to call sinners, not the self-righteous" (Mark 2:14–17).

### *The Common People*

Of course, most of the people in Palestine at the time of Christ were "none of the above." They were not experts in the law or leaders of the Sanhedrin. They were just people who struggled to obey the Torah or who had given up on the ancient promises of their fathers. Mostly, they were people who were too preoccupied with the daily business of survival to give much thought to the religious quarrels of their day.

*Women*

Women play an important role in the gospels, especially in light of their sociological standing at the time. Women were considered the property of men and were given few of the male privileges of the faith. They were excluded from the study of the Torah, were not allowed into the same places of prayer, could not read from the scrolls, and simply were considered inferior to men in every way. Yet the gospels give them a prominent role in discipleship. Jesus refused to condemn the sinful women who were the victims of male chauvinist laws which allowed adulterous women to be stoned to death but called for no such penalty for men. Martha and Mary were friends of Jesus. Luke portrays a woman, Mary the mother of Jesus, as the ideal Christian. It was women who were present at the death of Christ, and it was his women disciples who discovered his empty tomb. There is no doubt that Jesus' attitude toward women transcended the attitudes of his time and culture.

*Life of the Early Church*

In addition to knowing some of the historical and cultural background of Palestine at the time of Christ, it is also important to be familiar with some of the major issues in the life of the early church. As we said earlier, the gospels were written decades after Christ's death and resurrection, and much of what is contained in them reflects the situation of the primitive Christian communities.

## The Parousia

As we have already seen, the Jewish expectation of the Messiah included the idea of the coming of the reign of God, the final fulfillment of God's saving plan for his people. Thus, **the early church believed that the end was near. They thought that the resurrection of Jesus would soon be followed by the establishment of God's kingdom in its fullness.** They not only believed that Jesus would return but they prayed for it. This second coming of Christ is called the parousia and with it would come Christ's final victory over the powers of sin and death.

As time passed on, the parousia became a more difficult issue. In the earliest New Testament document, the first letter of Paul to the Thessalonians (51 A.D.), Paul is responding to the fears of the Christians of Thessalonica who are concerned about those who have died before the return of Christ. Although Paul reassures them, it is obvious that he still believes that the parousia is imminent and will take place within his lifetime.

The gospels seem to give conflicting information about the parousia. On the one hand, there are passages that seem to indicate that the parousia is about to dawn. It will occur before the apostles have the chance to preach to all the towns of Israel (Matthew 10:23). It will happen before the present generation passes away (Matthew 24:34). Yet no one knows the day nor the hour not even Jesus himself (Matthew 24:36). These passages reflect the situation of the early church as it waits hopefully for the coming of Christ. History has shown that the hopes of the early church were misplaced. Nearly two thousand years later we continue to await the coming of God's kingdom in its fullness. It may be a thousand years away. Or ten million years away. Or a week from Tuesday. The gospels do not give us any hidden, symbolic clues to know the answer (as some preachers like to pretend). They do reflect the church's concern with this important issue.

The delay of the parousia also made the church face another important issue: What was the role of the church in the world? If the future of the church was going to be much longer than originally anticipated, what should the mission of the church entail?

## *The Early Church: Jew and Gentile*

In the twentieth century, we think of the Jewish and Christian religions as being two very separate faiths. Yet in the early church, this was not the case. It was possible to be both Jewish and Christian. Jesus was a Jew and he saw his mission as one that belonged to Israel. The apostles, disciples, his mother and friends were all Jewish. Likewise the first Christians were all Jewish. They did not envision their faith in Jesus as a contradiction to their lifelong faith. They did not believe that they were converting to a new religion. As far as they were concerned, there was no contradiction between being Jewish and following Jesus who was the messiah of Israel. For the same reasons, the Jewish authorities saw Christianity as an heretical Jewish sect and falling under their authority to discipline.

Before too long, Jewish Christianity was faced with a dilemma. Gentiles were responding to the message about Jesus and receiving the gift of the Holy Spirit. Must these Gentile converts take on the faith and laws of Israel as well as believe in Jesus? Was it necessary for the Gentiles to obey the Mosaic law including circumcision and the dietary laws? At stake in the issue was a very critical point: Would Christianity be open to cultures other than Judaism or would it continue to see itself as a branch of Jewish faith?

The debate within the church consisted of three basic positions:

1. Those who believed that the followers of Jesus must follow the Mosaic law in its entirety. This group was made up of Christians who were formerly Pharisaic Jews who became known as Judaizers.

2. Those who believed that some elements of the Mosaic law should be preserved and obeyed by the Gentile Christians. These consisted mostly of dietary laws and laws against sexual immorality. Included in this compromise position were two of the great leaders of the early church: Peter and James.

3. Those who believed that baptism and faith in Christ were the only essential elements to being a Christian. Obedience of the Mosaic law was not wrong but it was unnecessary. This group was best represented by St. Paul.

Initially, the second group won out. Various leaders of the church met in Jerusalem to discuss the issue and reached the compromise position. In time, however, the third position prevailed as Christianity became a faith that was predominantly Gentile and lost its Jewish character.

## Summary

1. In order to understand Jesus and the gospels we must understand the world in which he lived and in which the gospels were written.
2. During the ministry of Jesus, Palestine was under the control of Rome.
3. Hopes for a messiah centered mostly around a political/religious figure who would restore Israel to its former glory.
4. There was a wide variety of groups and beliefs within Judaism at the time of Jesus. Scribes and Pharisees were the most devout Jews. Sadducees were a priestly class who exercised both religious and political power. Zealots were Jewish nationalists intent on overthrowing Roman rule.

5. Samaritans and tax collectors were among the most hated by the Jews: Samaritans for their heretical activities and tax collectors for their collaboration with the Romans.
6. The temple in Jerusalem was the center of Jewish faith where sacrifice was offered to God and where pilgrims journeyed for the great feasts.
7. The Torah was the heart of everyday Jewish life. Obedience to the law brought a man on the path to righteousness.
8. The early church expected Jesus to return imminently and were forced to rethink their mission in light of the delay.
9. The church was originally entirely Jewish Christian and only in time opened its doors to other cultures and traditions, thus altering the makeup of the church forever.

## Study Questions

1. What nation occupied Palestine at the time of Christ? Why was foreign occupation so devastating to the Jews?

2. Where did the notion of the messiah originate? How was Jesus different than the expectations of his day?

3. Describe each of the following: Pharisees, Sadducees, scribes, Essenes, Samaritans, zealots. Can you think of any contemporary characters similar to each of these?

4. What was the difference between the temple and the synagogue?

5. What was the Torah? What were some of the different attitudes toward it by the people living during the time of Jesus?

6. What did early Christians believe about the end of the world?

7. What was the "Gentile" problem faced by the early church? How was it resolved?

# 3

# The Coming of the Reign of God

From a strictly historical point of view, it would be hard to argue with the thesis that no one has had more of an effect on western civilization than Jesus Christ. Yet, who Jesus was and what he stood for has been interpreted in a thousand diverse ways, often to justify a thousand diverse activities. The understanding of the person and message of Christ has often reflected the piety and culture of a given period more than it has reflected the actual words and deeds of Christ. Each age has, however, had those saints and seers who have been faithful to the gospel. Christian history is filled with the lives of those who have brought the spirit of Christ and the gospels to every age. It has also been covered by a shadow, a dark side, by those who have turned the cross into a sword or the gospel into a tool for intolerance and persecution. Certainly, if the church is to be taken seriously in the future as a voice of hope, of peace and of truth, it must be rooted in the gospel. Its meaning must be rooted in the meaning of Christ. There is no better place to begin the search for the spirit and message of Christ than in the gospels.

The first three chapters have been devoted to laying the groundwork for reading the gospels. Beginning with this chapter, we get into the gospels themselves. There are two ways to read them: first, with the detachment and objectivity of the scholar, and, second, with the openness and receptivity of the seeker. We must learn to do both. To do only the first misses the point of why the gospels were written in the first place: to enable people to encounter the spirit of the risen Christ. To do only the second runs the risk of blindly projecting our own meanings and agenda into the gospel.

We will begin in this chapter with an examination of the core message of Jesus Christ. If you were to ask most Christians what this message was, they would probably say "to love one another." It's hard to find fault in that because the mandate to love certainly was central to the message of Jesus. In fact, however, **the theme of love was one of several in the larger proclamation of the coming of the reign of God.** Mark's summary statement will serve as the basis for this chapter: "Jesus appeared in Galilee proclaiming the good news of God: 'This is the time of fulfillment. The reign of God is at hand! Reform your lives and believe in the gospel!'" (Mark 1:14b–15).

## *This Is the Time of Fulfillment*

In the movie *Hannah and Her Sisters,* the character played by Woody Allen believes that he has a terminal disease. Upon discovering that this is not the case, he is filled with a new life and enthusiasm. He smiles, he skips, and he takes on the exuberance of a child. Suddenly, he stops. His joy is gone. He is not going to die—now. But he will die someday. He has been given more time, but what is the point of the time? Woody Allen, in his own inimitable and humorous fashion, has asked the viewer a very serious question—namely, what's the point? **Is there any meaning or purpose to the passage of time on earth?** This is perhaps the most fundamental religious question that can be asked, and it is central to the message of Christ. Jesus sees himself ushering in a time of fulfillment.

**The history of Israel and its faith is one that is based on promise:** the promise to Abraham to have descendants as numerous as the stars in the sky; the promise to Moses that God would free his people from slavery; the promise to David that his throne shall reign forever; the promise of Isaiah that God had not abandoned his people; the promise of Jeremiah that God would establish a new covenant with his people; the promise of shalom when the lion and the lamb would lie down together. Israel awaited the fulfillment of God's promises. For them, Yahweh was a God who had actively invaded time and history. Yahweh was a God who was present to them and who accomplished great things for them. The march of time was going somewhere and it was being led by God himself. To return to the question asked by Woody Allen, the passage of time indeed had meaning and found its meaning in the fulfillment of God's promises. According to Jesus, the time had come. The fulfillment is now!

In the Greek translation of the Hebrew Scriptures (called the Septuagint) we find two words to designate time: **chronos** and **kairos**. Chronos is the simple passage of time as it is ordinarily experienced (from whence we get the word "chronology"). Kairos is special time. It is the time of God's intervention, his revelation and salvation. Kairos is time filled with meaning, alive with spirit and insight. In the world of everyday experience, we could say that most of our time at work and with out families is chronos. Falling in love, getting married, the birth of a child, is kairos. When Jesus says, "This is the time of fulfillment," he is talking about the kairos of God. Time itself has reached its pinnacle and fulfillment. The God who has been revealing himself to the people of Israel is now about to act in a unique and special way. Throughout the

Hebrew Scriptures, Yahweh has been involved in the process of drawing his people nearer to him. This process will now find its fulfillment in Jesus. Luke makes this point clearly in the story of Jesus' return to his hometown of Nazareth and his teaching in the synagogue:

> He came to Nazareth where he had been reared, and entering the synagogue on the sabbath as he was in the habit of doing, he stood up to do the reading. When the book of the prophet Isaiah was handed to him, he unrolled the scroll and found the passage where it was written:
>
> "The spirit of the Lord is upon me;
>     therefore he has anointed me.
> He has sent me to bring glad tidings to the poor,
>     to proclaim liberty to captives,
> Recovery of sight to the blind
>     and release to prisoners,
> To announce a year of favor from the Lord."
>
> Rolling up the scroll he gave it back to the assistant and sat down. All in the synagogue had their eyes fixed on him. Then he began by saying to them, **"Today this Scripture passage is fulfilled in your hearing"** (Luke 4:16–21).

Jesus does not see himself as simply another prophet in a long line of prophets. Instead here he identifies himself with a very spiritual notion of God's "anointed one" (messiah) who announces a "year of favor," a special time. In fulfilling this passage of Scripture, Luke portrays Jesus as fulfilling the promises of God.

## *The Time Is Now*

In addition to emphasizing the notion of the fulfillment of God's promises, there is also an urgency in Jesus' message that consistently comes across in the gospels. Because this is a unique time of fulfillment, Jesus is concerned that the people of Palestine are going to miss it. We continually see Jesus making appeals to the people: Wake up! Be alert! The time is now!

> He said to the crowds: "When you see a cloud rising in the west, you say immediately that rain is coming—and so it does. When the wind blows from the south, you say it is going to be hot—and so it is. You hypocrites! If you can interpret the portents of earth and sky, why can you not interpret the present time?" (Luke 12:54–56).

Jesus' point is clear: while the people have learned to interpret the signs of nature they are unable to interpret the signs of God's presence. Now is the time of fulfillment—and they are going to miss it!

## *The Reign of God Is at Hand!*

When Jesus proclaimed the coming of the reign of God, he was not inventing a new religious idea but using one that appears in the Hebrew Scriptures. The reign of God (or the kingdom of God, as it is also translated) is a phrase that does not appear often in the Hebrew Scriptures but its meaning can be tied to a number of different concepts. God's reign is made manifest through human submission to his will. It is accomplished through the power of God in his relationship to his people Israel. It concerns God's judgment and his establishment of Israel as the light to the Gentiles. It was related to the day of Yahweh when God would reveal himself in all his glory and judge all the nations of the earth. In some parts of the Scriptures, the reign of God seems to be a reality closely associated with this world. It will mean the end of war, pestilence and disease. It will have material and political blessings. In other parts of the Hebrew Scriptures, the idea seems more closely tied to an **eschatological kingdom** (that is, a kingdom that will be at the end of human history and will close human history).

In view of these different notions, when Jesus proclaimed the arrival of the reign of God, the proclamation probably meant different things to different people. Although Jesus used this phrase, he would fill it with his own meaning, for his understanding of the kingdom was related to the past notion but also distinct from it. At no point does Jesus formally spell out what he means by the reign of God. He does not treat it like a theological treatise but as a spiritual reality that can only be understood through the eyes of faith. We will focus on six important themes that can be discovered in Jesus' teaching about the reign of God.

1. *The reign of God is brought about by the power of God.* The reign of God is not a human achievement or program or religion. It is very simply the power of God among human beings. As such, **it is capable of growth and transformation far beyond any human calculations.** The stories of the mustard seed and the leaven bring out precisely this point:

> "The reign of God is like a mustard seed which someone took and sowed in his field. It is the smallest seed of all, yet when full-grown it is the largest of plants. It becomes so big a shrub that the birds in the sky come build their nests in its branches."

He offered them still another image: "The reign of God is like yeast which a woman took and kneaded into three measures of flour. Eventually, the whole mass of dough began to rise (Matthew 13:31–33).

Jesus uses two commonplace images: one from nature and another from the household. The images have one thing in common. There is a disproportionate growth that takes place in both the plant and the flour. The power of God, like the seed and the leaven, is able to bring about remarkable, seemingly impossible, transformation.

2. *The reign of God is both a present and a future reality.* One of the peculiar characteristics of the reign of God is that it seems to be something that Jesus speaks of as both a present and a future reality. He says that the kingdom is "at hand" yet he instructs his disciples to pray for its coming (in the Lord's Prayer: "thy kingdom come"). This theme is present throughout the gospels. For this reason, Scripture scholars refer to the "already ... but not yet" quality of the kingdom. It has broken through into the world but has not yet reached its fullness.

Today, the reign of God is more often thought of as a reality that occurs after death or at the end of time. We have a tendency to downplay the *now* quality of the kingdom. Religions that emphasize a reward and punishment motif ("be good and you will go to heaven") seem to think of God's reign as almost entirely outside this world and its history. That, however, is a very limited version of the gospel picture. There are other people who see faith as having to do only with the way we live in this world without any future reference to an "endtime" ("you make your own heaven or hell here on earth" seems to be their calling card). Again, this seems to be an incomplete picture of the gospel message. Jesus' notion of the kingdom is clearly one that is presently at work transforming lives and history, and yet one that will only be complete in God's time. The story of the weeds makes this point:

> "The reign of God may be likened to a man who sowed good seed in his field. While everyone was asleep, his enemy came and sowed weeds through his wheat, and then made off. When the crop began to mature and yield grain, the weeds made their appearance as well. The owner's slaves came to him and said, 'Sir, did you not sow good seed in your field? Where are the weeds coming from?' He answered, 'I see an enemy's hand in this.' His slaves said to him, 'Do you want us to go out and pull them up?' 'No,' he replied, 'pull up the weeds and you might take the wheat along with them. Let them grow together until harvest; then at harvest time, I will order the harvesters, First collect the weeds and bundle them up to burn, then gather the wheat into my barn' " (Matthew 13:24–30).

From this story it is clear that there are two "kingdoms" at work here on earth: the kingdom of God and another kingdom in opposition to God's (known biblically as "the kingdom of sin and death"). It will only be in the end that the kingdom of God is freed from all encounter with sin. This story exemplifies Jesus' teaching about the kingdom: it is already present, but its completion lies in God's future.

3. *God is near to us in love.* One of the great characteristics of Yahweh in the Hebrew Scriptures is his **transcendence** or his infinite greatness. His ways are not man's ways.

He is the Creator, the Lord of heaven and earth. He is the Holy One whose name cannot be uttered. Jesus certainly recognizes the transcendence of God, but he emphasizes his **immanence,** his nearness to us. The stories that Jesus uses to describe God are commonplace ones using details from the most ordinary aspects of human life. Even more telling than that, however, is the name that Jesus uses to describe God: **Abba.** The word Abba comes from Jesus' native **Aramaic.** It was a word used by children for their father that might best be rendered "Dad" or "Daddy" in English. It is a term of warmth, affection and closeness. If it were possible to summarize the message of Jesus in just one word, the best word to choose would be Abba. The implications of the word are staggering. The Lord of the universe, the ineffable mystery of God, is also Abba. When we look out at the vastness of the created world, when we allow our imaginations and intellect to seek the ground and source of that world, we are to call it Daddy. Of course, the word Abba not only tells us something about God, it tells us something about ourselves as well. We are God's children and therefore brother and sister to each other. This name lies at the heart of the good news: God is Abba! That is good news indeed!

4. *The reign of God offers peace and reconciliation.* We have already seen a number of ways in which Jesus did not fit into the expectations of the people of his time. Perhaps the most striking peculiarity of Jesus was his association with sinners and outcasts. The most devout, religious people of the day, the Pharisees, were baffled by such behavior. They had scrupulously obeyed God's law and were now being told that God's grace and pardon were being offered to all.

> While Jesus was reclining to eat in Levi's house, many tax collectors and those known as sinners

## The Parables

If the main thrust of Jesus' teaching and preaching was the coming of the reign of God, then the parables were the special vehicle through which he communicated his message. By now we should be well aware that not every word placed in the mouth of Jesus by the evangelists was actually spoken by him. Through the oral tradition and the editorial revamping of the authors, the words of Jesus are often shaped to meet the needs of the audience. To capture the actual words of Jesus, we can do no better than to begin with the parables. These stories and illustrations are truly unique. Nothing exactly like them can be found anywhere else in the Scriptures. **The stories reflect the local color of the culture in which Jesus lived:** Jesus speaks of farmers sowing seed and women kneading dough, of farmers hiring workers and shepherds seeking lost sheep. And **they are directed to the problems that Jesus confronted:** many of the parables are directed to the self-righteous Pharisees with whom Jesus so often struggled. The language of the parables, while written in Greek in the gospels, contain many Semitic expressions that would reflect the actual language of Jesus.

What is a parable?

This is not such an easy question to answer and some Scripture scholars differ on their estimation of what constitutes a parable. The Old Testament forerunner was called the *mashal*. The *mashal* referred to many different types of figures of speech: illustrations, allegories, metaphors, stories. The word parable comes from the Greek, *parabole*, meaning a comparison. A parable is most often a comparison between everyday affairs and the reign of God. **Each parable has one main point.** They are not allegories with hidden meanings. They were told by Jesus to the people of his time in order to help jolt them into a new way of perceiving life and God's relationship to his people. For that reason they often contained some kind of "twist" or element of surprise (for example, the Samaritan is the example of a loving neighbor; cf. Luke 10).

joined him and his disciples at dinner. The number of those who followed him was large. When the scribes who belonged to the Pharisee party saw that he was eating with tax collectors and offenders against the law, they complained to his disciples, "Why does he eat with such as these?" Overhearing the remark, Jesus said to them, **"People who are healthy do not need a doctor; sick people do. I have come to call sinners, not the self-righteous"** (Mark 2:15–17).

Jesus identifies himself as a doctor, one who brings healing and reconciliation. He eats at the home of a tax collector. Tax collectors felt the full wrath of the Pharisees. In addition to being notorious thieves, the tax collectors were the most vile of thieves because they collaborated with the Romans to make their money. Yet it was such as these that responded to Jesus' offer of mercy and reconciliation. Those who felt that they were not in need of healing would have no need for Jesus. Jesus' big problem with the Pharisees was that many of them seemed to believe that God "owed" them a reward for their virtue and resented the fact that sinners were being offered a pardon. The illusion of their own perfection made them fail to see their own sinfulness and need for healing.

5. *The love of God is a gift freely given.* If you believe that God loves you as a reward for your good behavior, then you also believe that you can control and manipulate God's love and that God parcels out love in small packages equal to our small deeds. If you believe these things, you would be similar to some of the Pharisees of Jesus' era. The conflict between Jesus and the Pharisees was not a trivial one. It focused on the very understanding of what God was like in relation to human beings. Central to Jesus' understanding of

God as Abba was the belief that he freely, graciously and superabundantly lavishes his people with his love and mercy. His love is a gift. It is not something that we could ever earn.

It was in response to this problem with the Pharisees that Jesus told the often-misunderstood story of the laborers in the vineyard:

> "The reign of God is like the case of an owner of an estate who went out at dawn to hire workmen for his vineyard. After reaching an agreement with them for the usual daily wage, he sent them out to his vineyard. He came out about midmorning and saw other men standing around the marketplace without work, so he said to them, 'You too go along to my vineyard and I will pay you whatever is fair.' He came out again around noon and midafternoon and did the same. Finally going out in the late afternoon he found still others standing around. To these he said, 'Why have you been standing here idle all day?' 'No one has hired us,' they told him. He said, 'You go to the vineyard too.' When evening came the owner of the vineyard said to his foreman, 'Call the workmen and give them their pay, but begin with the last group and end with the first.' When those hired late in the afternoon came up they received a full day's pay, and when the first group appeared they supposed they would get more; yet they received the same daily wage. Thereupon they complained to the owner, 'This last group did only an hour's work, but you have put them on the same basis as us who have worked a full day in the scorching heat.' 'My friend,' he said to one in reply, 'I do you no injustice. You agreed on the usual wage, did you not? Take your pay and go home. I intend to

give this man who was hired last the same pay as you. I am free to do as I please with my money, am I not? Or are you envious because I am generous?' " (Matthew 20:1–15).

In order to understand this story it is important to remember that Jesus is not trying to teach a lesson in business practices. He is trying to explain the reign of God. The story again relates to Jesus' practice of associating with sinners and outcasts. Like those who were hired late in the day, they have received a gift based not on their performance but on the generosity of the giver. Those who would begrudge them the gift, or feel that they have "earned" more, do not understand the love of God and show little sign of having been touched by that love.

6. *God's reign demands a decision from us.* In light of the last two sections, it might seem that we need not do anything good and that it makes no difference: God will always forgive us. Of course, that is not the message of Christ. His proclamation of God's love and mercy confronts us with the most basic decision: How will I respond to such news? Jesus did not encourage the tax collectors and sinners to continue sinning. To the contrary, **he called them to a new way of life in light of God's love for them.** The story of the gospel is not only the story of God's grace; it is also the story of our response. The offer of God's grace is meaningless if we are not open to it, if we are unwilling to respond to the offer. This demands commitment to following Christ. It means being able to let go of a life focused around one's own needs and satisfactions. It calls for the difficult task of letting go:

Another time a man came up to him and said, "Teacher, what good must I do to possess everlasting life?" ... He answered, "If you wish to enter into life keep the commandments." ... The young man said to him, "I have kept all these; what do I need to do further?" Jesus told him, "If you seek perfection, go sell your possessions, and give to the poor. You will then have treasure in heaven. Afterward come back and follow me." Hearing these words, the young man went away sad, for his possessions were many (Matthew 19:16,17b,20–22).

This story has often been misinterpreted to mean that Christians must not have any possessions or that the man in the story fails to achieve salvation. It means neither of those, but it does show us the nature of the reign of God. It confronts us with the most fundamental decisions about our lives. When all is said and done, where do my true allegiances lie? What is the real number one priority in my life? Commitment to God's offer means that life can never be the same again:

The reign of God is like a buried treasure which a man found in a field. He hid it again and rejoicing in his find went out and sold all that he had and bought that field (Matthew 13:44).

The discovery of God's love is a source of great joy—a discovered treasure—but it means giving up old ways and false gods!

*"Reform Your Lives"*

Jesus' proclamation of the good news of God's love and mercy is certainly a message that is easy and comforting to hear. The good news does not end there, however. We have not heard the good news if we have not also heard the call to reform our lives. This part of the message is more of a challenge than a comfort. We are in need of reform. There is something out of whack inside of us. The word that is used in the gospel of Mark is **metanoete,** a Greek word that means to change one's entire perspective, one's most basic consciousness. This "metanoia" is best rendered in English as "conversion" or "change of heart." It entails a fundamental redirection of our lives. It means no longer seeing the world from the self-serving perspective of the ego, but seeing the world as the domain of God. It means ceasing to build our own "kingdoms" and cooperating in building God's. There is a wonderful story in John's gospel about how Jesus' call to conversion includes both sinners and the righteous:

> The scribes and the Pharisees led a woman forward who had been caught in adultery. They made her stand there in front of everyone. "Teacher," they said to him, "this woman has been caught in the act of adultery. In the law, Moses ordered such women to be stoned. What do you have to say about the case?" ... Jesus bent down and started tracing on the ground with his finger. When they persisted in their questioning, he straightened up and said to them, "Let the man among you who has no sin be the first to cast a stone at her." A second time he bent down and wrote on the ground. Then the audience drifted away one by one, beginning with the elders. This left him alone with the woman, who continued to stand there before him. Jesus finally straightened up and said to her, "Woman, where did they all disappear to? Has no one condemned you?" "No one, sir," she answered. Jesus said, "Nor do I condemn you.

You may go. But from now on, avoid this sin" (John 8:3–11).

In this story, Jesus calls the men to a new way of seeing themselves and this woman. She is not the sinner and they the righteous. They are all sinners in need of conversion. The men are forced to abandon their stones and their stony hearts.

It is possible to read the gospels as the stories of those who respond to the challenge of conversion and those who fail to respond. It is important to remember that conversion is also "good news." Although difficult and challenging it leads to a new life—one that brings with it the joy of the kingdom. Of course, the gospel story is one that continues today. The call to conversion is still a challenge. It still demands letting go of all the reasons, real and imagined, why we cannot change.

*"Believe in the Gospel"*

Faith: the final component in the good news of Jesus. What does Jesus mean when he says, "Believe in the gospel"? Two thousand years later it can be difficult to recapture the spirit of his words. In an age when we are born into our faith, baptized as infants and brought to church as children, being "Catholic" or "Protestant" or "Christian" may say no more about us than the color of our eyes or hair: they are simple facts of our existence. Do any of these labels really mean that we "believe in the gospel"? Today when we think of "faith" we often think of the acceptance of a certain set of creeds and rules that make up part of a faith.

For Jesus, to "believe in the gospel" meant to personally accept him as the one who brings salvation. It is to see in Christ the power of God at work. There were many reasons why people could not believe this. To those who lived in Nazareth, he was "the carpenter's son," the boy that they watched grow up (see Mark 6:1–6). For the Pharisees and scribes, he was a threat to the true ways of God and the law of Moses. To the zealots, he was a romantic idealist who preached love of enemies. To "believe in the gospel" means to align oneself with Christ and to become his disciple. It is to allow the power of Christ to transform your life.

## *The Miracles of Jesus: The Power of the Kingdom at Work*

Jesus not only spoke about the reign of God, his actions manifested that reign. Jesus embodied God's kingdom in which human beings were reconciled with God. During his lifetime, there were two things that Jesus did that were unique agents of the reign of God: he forgave sins and he performed miracles. A story in Mark brings out the meaning of both of these actions:

> He came back to Capernaum after a lapse of several days and word got around that he was home. At that they began to gather in great numbers. There no longer was any room for them, even around the door. While he was delivering God's word to them, some people arrived bringing a paralyzed man to him. The four who carried him were unable to bring him to Jesus because of the crowd, so they began to open up the roof over the spot where Jesus was. When they had made a hole, they let down the mat on which the paralyzed man was lying. When Jesus saw their faith, he said to the paralyzed man, "My son, your sins are forgiven." Now some of the scribes were sitting there asking themselves, "Why does the man talk in this way? He commits blas-

phemy! Who can forgive sins except God alone?" Jesus was immediately aware of their reasoning, though they kept it to themselves, and he said to them: "Why do you harbor these thoughts? Which is easier, to say to the paralytic, 'Your sins are forgiven,' or to say, 'Stand up, pick up your mat, and walk again'? That you may know that the Son of Man has authority on earth to forgive sins" (he said to the paralyzed man), "I command you: Stand up! Pick up your mat and go home." The man stood and picked up his mat and went outside in the sight of everyone. They were awestruck; all gave praise to God, saying, "We have never seen anything like this!" (Mark 2:1–12).

In this passage, Mark links together the meaning of the miracle and the forgiveness of sins. In those days, the Jewish people believed that physical maladies were punishment for sins committed. Thus, the paralytic would have probably seen himself cut off from God's favor. Jesus goes to the root of the issue and says to him, "Your sins are forgiven." Jesus is not like a prophet proclaiming God's mercy on sinners. He takes on the power to forgive, an act which no man would have the right to do. And this is precisely the point: Jesus is not just any man or even a great man. He alone can forgive sins because he alone embodies the mercy of God.

In order to show the scribes that he has the power to forgive, Jesus cures the paralytic. It is in this context that the miracles of Jesus are to be understood. They are instruments of God's reign in which all shall be made whole. Sickness, as well as sin, is a sign of the human need to be healed. The miracles of Jesus reveal that through him God's reign has broken into the world.

Stories of Jesus performing miracles can be traced to the

earliest preaching of the church and have an historical basis. This does not mean, however, that every miracle mentioned in the gospels happened exactly as described. To the contrary, the evangelists felt free to adapt and enhance miracle stories in order to teach their communities about Jesus.

## Summary

1. The main theme of the preaching of Jesus was the coming of the reign of God.
2. The early church understood Jesus as the fulfillment of the promises of Yahweh and of the faith of Israel.
3. Jesus was not simply another prophet but the definitive offer of God's salvation in history.
4. The reign of God has already begun in history but it remains incomplete and will find its fulfillment in the eschatological kingdom.
5. God's reign is brought about by God. It is not the same as human achievement (although it certainly does not exclude it).
6. Jesus calls God "Abba," an Aramaic word meaning Daddy, and thus emphasizes the nearness of God.
7. God's love need not be earned—it is a gift freely given.
8. God's love demands a response, a conversion, on our part.

## Questions for Review

1. In what sense is the faith of Israel based on promise? How did the early church understand Jesus in relationship to those promises?

2. Why is Jesus more than another prophet?

3. In what sense is the reign of God a present reality?

Give some examples from your own experience on how this might be true.

4. What is the main point of the story of the mustard seed and the leaven?

5. What word does Jesus use to describe God? What does it mean and what is its significance?

6. What is the main point of the story of the laborers in the vineyard?

7. What is the gospel notion of conversion?

# 4

# The Synoptic Gospels

**Mark**

**Scholars generally agree that Mark's gospel was the first written (ca. 70 A.D.)** approximately thirty-five to forty years after the death and resurrection of Jesus. It is the shortest of the four gospels, the least theologically sophisticated, and written in the most simple Greek. Mark's gospel seems to lack some of the bold strokes of genius found in Matthew (e.g., the Sermon on the Mount) or Luke (the parables of the prodigal son and the good Samaritan) or John (the prologue and the last discourse), but his gospel presents a very powerful and important understanding of Jesus. Because it was the first written, it merits a special place of importance. While the letters of Paul were written before Mark, it is in Mark that we find the earliest portrayal of the teaching and message of Jesus, the conflicts in his life, his relationship to his followers, and the nature of his death and resurrection.

*The Messianic Secret*

Mark's gospel centers around the theme of the "messianic secret." It is important to recall that most people in Palestine at the time of Christ thought that the messiah would be coming in power to establish the reign of God. Jesus is the messiah but not the kind that the people are expecting, and so for that reason his identity must remain a secret that will only be gradually revealed. However, the secret of Jesus' identity is not a secret to the reader who is informed from the start that Jesus is the Son of God, the messiah: "Here begins the gospel of Jesus Christ, the Son of God" (Mark 1:1). Mark is intent on showing that within his lifetime Jesus was profoundly misunderstood, and that if the reader is to accept Jesus as the Christ he must learn exactly what type of Messiah he is: one who offers suffering love as salvation.

Scholars differ in their assessment of how Mark's gospel is best outlined and structured. We will use the most basic and obvious outline in Mark.

*Chapters 1–8:26: The Mystery of Jesus*

The first eleven verses reveal to the reader who Jesus is: "Here begins the gospel of Jesus Christ, the Son of God" (Mark 1:1). Mark makes no mention of Jesus' birth. Rather he begins with Jesus' baptism by John in the Jordan. This marks the beginning of Jesus' public ministry, and Mark wants to make clear the messianic character of this ministry. Thus at the baptism of Jesus we hear the words of the Father: "You are my beloved Son. On you my favor rests" (Mark 1:11).

While the reader is made aware of Jesus' divine mission, those who encounter him fail to understand him. The next eight chapters (half the gospel) continually ask the question, "who is Jesus?" Jesus does not fit into any of the categories that people have. The people are taken up with him, but do not know what to make of him: "The people were spellbound by his teaching because he taught with authority and not like the scribes" (Mark 1:22). When Jesus cured a man possessed by an evil spirit, "all who looked on were amazed. They began to ask one another: 'What does this mean?'" (Mark 1:27a).

Upon healing a paralytic, Mark reports: "They were awestruck; all gave praise to God saying, 'We have never seen anything like this!' " (Mark 2:12b). And upon healing a deaf mute, "their amazement went beyond all bounds: 'He has done everything well! He makes the deaf hear and the mute speak!' " (Mark 7:37).

Nor is it only the common people that are baffled by Jesus. The Pharisees and scribes also fail to understand Jesus and reject his behavior as blasphemous. When Jesus forgives the sins of the paralytic, "the scribes were sitting there asking themselves: 'Why does the man talk in that way? He commits blasphemy! Who can forgive sins except God alone?' " (Mark 2:6–7). They also reject his attitude toward sinners and the law. When Jesus eats with tax collectors, the Pharisees are scandalized, "Why does he eat with such as these?" they ask his disciples. The Pharisees go so far as to say that "he is possessed by Beelzebul" (Mark 3:22).

**Mark emphasizes that even his family and disciples did not truly understand him.** In one of the most extraordinary lines in the gospels, the evangelist writes that when Jesus was hemmed in by the crowds and unable to get any food, his family heard of this and "they came to take charge of him, saying, 'He is out of his mind' " (Mark 3:21). Even some of Jesus' relatives thought that he was crazy. His disciples consistently do not understand Jesus' teaching or the source of his power. When Jesus calms the storm on the sea, the disciples ask one another, "Who can this be that the wind and the sea obey him?" (Mark 5:41b). When Jesus multiplies the loaves and walks on water, "they were taken aback by these happenings, for they did not understand about the loaves. On the contrary, their minds were completely closed to the meaning of the events" (Mark 6:51b–52).

Running parallel with the theme of the people's amazement, confusion and misunderstanding is Jesus' own desire to keep secret his identity and role. The only ones who seem to know Jesus' identity, other than the reader, are the demons. Because they are supernatural, they are aware of Jesus' supernatural origins. Yet Mark asserts that Jesus "would not permit the demons to speak, because they knew him" (Mark 1:34b), and "he kept ordering them sternly not to reveal who he was" (Mark 3:12). Likewise, Jesus often follows a cure with orders to keep it a secret. Upon healing a leper, he instructs him, "Not a word to anyone now" (Mark 1:44a).

The theme of the messianic secret reaches its climax in Mark 8:27–30. This begins a new division within Mark in which Jesus begins to reveal himself as the messiah who suffers and dies for his people. Jesus, the source of much confusion and bewilderment, now turns the question of his identity to his apostles:

> Then Jesus and his disciples set out for the villages around Caesarea Philippi. On the way, he asked his disciples this question: "Who do people say that I am?" They replied, "Some, John the Baptizer, others, Elijah, still others, one of the prophets." "And you," he went on to ask, "who do you say that I am?" Peter answered him, "You are the Messiah!" Then he gave them strict orders not to tell anyone about him (Mark 8:27–30).

Peter has correctly identified Jesus as the messiah but this is not yet to be public information. The reason for the secrecy becomes apparent in the next passage in Mark. **Jesus is the messiah but he is radically different than the messiah that people are expecting, including Peter:**

> He began to teach them that the Son of Man had to suffer much, be rejected by the elders, the chief

## Titles of Christ in the Synoptic Gospels

**Rabbi or Teacher.** The disciples of Jesus would have referred to him most often as "rabbi" (rabbouni) or "teacher" (*didaskolos*). These were honorary titles that contained no significant theological meaning.

**Son of Man.** In the gospels, it is Jesus who applies this enigmatic title to himself more than any other. It can be found fourteen times in Mark, thirty in Matthew and twenty-five in Luke. It is most likely borrowed from Daniel 7:13 where it symbolizes Israel in its future glory. Thus, the Son of Man is associated with the final age of salvation. Scripture scholars debate whether the title actually belongs to the earthly Jesus or was designated by the early church. If Jesus did use it (as many believe), it might have been chosen for its open-ended status: there were no clear expectations of who this character would be.

**Messiah** (Christ). This title refers to the "anointed" of Israel who would fulfill the messianic hopes of the nation. As we have already seen, the notion of the messiah was closely linked to nationalistic as well as religious hopes. It is questionable whether Jesus ever used the title himself within his own earthly ministry. If he did, it was only with great reservation because he did not establish a kingdom, nor was he gloriously triumphant, nor had he delivered Israel from the hands of the Gentiles. Yet it was as a false messiah that Jesus was crucified.

**Son of David.** All three synoptic gospels refer to Jesus as the Son of David because of the link between the line of David and the messiah (2 Samuel 7:14ff). It is not surprising that Matthew, emphasizing the link between Jesus and Jewish faith, should use it most often, including the opening line of the gospel: "A family record of Jesus Christ, son of David, son of Abraham."

**Lord.** The title "Lord" had two singularly different meanings. As used by Jesus' disciples, it would have meant "sir" or "master." However, after the resurrection, the title Lord was core to the proclamation of faith in Jesus. The Greek *kyrios,* "lord," was used in the Septuagint (Greek Old Testament) to translate Yahweh. Thus, "Lord" referred to Jesus' risen union with the Father, as Peter proclaims at Pentecost: "Therefore let the whole house of Israel know beyond any doubt that God has made both Lord and Messiah this Jesus whom you crucified" (Acts 2:36). Only Luke, of the three synoptic authors, refers to Jesus as Lord in this post-resurrectional sense.

priests and the scribes, be put to death and rise three days later. He said these things quite openly. Peter then took him aside and began to remonstrate with him. At this he turned around and, eyeing the disciples, reprimanded Peter: "Get out of my sight, you satan! You are not judging by God's standards but by man's!" (Mark 8:31–33).

Peter's expectations are like those of most of the people. He is looking for a powerful, triumphant messiah and Jesus will not be that. From this point on, Jesus will emphasize the cost involved in following him: "If a man wishes to come after me, he must deny his very self, take up his cross, and follow in my steps. Whoever would preserve his life will lose it, but whoever loses his life for my sake and the gospel's will preserve it" (Mark 8:34b–35). Jesus has now begun the process that will reveal the nature of his mission: he will go to Jerusalem. Ultimately, it is on the cross that Jesus is fully revealed as messiah. Ironically, this revelation is placed in the mouth of the pagan centurion: "Clearly this man was the Son of God" (Mark 15:39b).

## Matthew

### *Jesus: The Fulfillment of the Hebrew Scriptures*

If one were to read Matthew after Mark, perhaps the most striking contrast would be the amount of the teaching of Jesus that Matthew includes. Mark's gospel focuses on the power and authority of Jesus revealed in his miracles and his suffering and death. **Matthew is more intent on portraying Jesus as the great teacher,** the new Moses who fulfills the Jewish law. Much of what is contained in Matthew has been shaped to specifically meet the needs of the community to which he is writing. As we have mentioned earlier, Matthew is most likely a Jewish Christian who is writing to a mixed community of believers (that is, Jewish and Gentile Christian, very possibly the city of Antioch). He is intent on showing that Jesus is the messiah, the fulfillment of the Old Testament and the true teacher of the Torah (law). When Matthew wrote his gospel, there was a great deal of animosity between Christians and Jews. The Christians had been expelled from the synagogues, the temple had been destroyed and Pharisaic Judaism was becoming an ever stronger element within the faith of Israel. **Matthew sought to show that there was no inherent contradiction between the faith of Israel and belief in Jesus as the messiah.**

In order to accomplish this, Matthew often cites passages from the Old Testament to validate that Jesus is the fulfillment of the faith of Israel. This is especially true in a situation that would seemingly contradict Jewish expectations of the messiah. For example, in Matthew's version of the infancy narratives (the stories of Jesus' birth), he includes five scriptural passages that he believes to be fulfilled in the birth of Jesus. Likewise, when he traces the genealogy of Jesus (Matthew 1:1–17), he carefully traces it through David and back to Abraham, the father of Jewish faith.

*The Sermon on the Mount*

Matthew's gospel revolves around five discourses of Jesus. Jesus is portrayed as a Jew who has not broken away from the law but who seeks the law's fulfillment. He is the great teacher who shows the true path of righteousness. This is apparent in the first and most famous of the discourses, the Sermon on the Mount (chapters 5–7). The sermon is a collection of the teachings and sayings of Jesus brought together by Matthew. It ranks among the most famous and universally revered pieces of religious literature in the world. In it, Jesus is compared to Moses. Just as Moses went up the mountain to bring down the law, so now Jesus climbs the mountain to fulfill the law. **One of the great insights of the sermon is on the importance of interior conversion in the heart, reaching beyond the minimal demands of the law.** Jesus seems to belong to a liberal tradition within Judaism that believed not only in the written law but in the oral interpretation of the law (a position consistent with the Pharisees with whom he so often fought about the proper interpretation). Throughout chapter 5, Matthew contrasts the written law with Jesus' interpretation. He uses the formula: "You have heard the commandment... what I say to you is...." For example, "You have heard the commandment imposed on your forefathers, 'You shall not commit murder; every murderer shall be liable to judgment.' What I say to you is: everyone who grows angry with his brother shall be answerable to the Sanhedrin" (Matthew 5:21–22); or again, "You have heard the commandment, 'You shall not commit adultery.' What I say to you is: anyone who looks lustfully at a woman has already committed adultery with her in his thoughts" (Matthew 5:27–28). Jesus does not say that the Torah is unimportant or wrong. But his interpretation of the Torah demands more than simple outward conformity. It demands that the law be written in one's heart as love: "Do not think that I have come to abolish the law and the prophets. I have come not to abolish them but to fulfill them" (Matthew 5:17).

*The Mission of the Church*

**The second of the discourses (chapter 10) clearly reflects Matthew's reworking of the material to fit the needs of his audience.** In it Jesus gives his apostles instruc-

> How blest are the poor in spirit:
>   the reign of God is theirs.
> Blest too are the sorrowing;
>   they shall be consoled.
> Blest are the lowly;
>   they shall inherit the land.
> Blest are they who hunger and thirst for holiness;
>   they shall have their fill.
> Blest are they who show mercy;
>   mercy shall be theirs.
> Blest are the single-hearted
>   for they shall see God.
> Blest too the peacemakers;
>   they shall be called children of God.
> Blest are those persecuted for holiness sake;
>   the reign of God is theirs.
> Blest are you when they insult you and persecute you and utter every kind of slander against you because of me.
> Be glad and rejoice, for your reward is great in heaven;
> They persecuted the prophets before you in the very same way.

tions for their mission, yet much of it mirrors the situation of the first century church: "They will hale you into court and flog you in their synagogues ("their" synagogues reflects the fact that the Christians were expelled from them). You will be brought to trial before rulers and kings, to give witness before them and before the Gentiles on my account" (Matthew 10:17–18). This passage reflects what did in fact happen in the early church, although Matthew makes it appear that the words are addressed by Jesus to the apostles to help them in their mission while Jesus was still alive. The apostles are the legitimate witnesses of faith in the early church: "He who welcomes you welcomes me" (10:40a), but the leaders of the church are to expect conflict. When Matthew writes, "Do not think that my mission on earth is to spread peace. My mission is to spread, not peace, but division" (10:34), he is aware of the great conflicts that have taken place in order to give birth to the church (Jew vs. Jewish Christian; Jewish Christian vs. Gentile Christian, to name just two).

*Parables of the Kingdom*

The third discourse (chapter 13) is made up of seven parables of the kingdom. Each of the parables is adaptable to the situation of Matthew's readers. The **parable of the seed** (Matthew 13:4–8), when originally told by Jesus, probably was meant to emphasize the overabounding generosity of the Father who sent his grace everywhere.

> One day a farmer went out sowing. Part of what he sowed landed on a footpath where birds came and ate it up. Part of it fell on rocky ground, where it had little soil. It sprouted at once since the soil had no depth, but when the sun rose and scorched it, it began to wither for lack of roots. Again part of the seed fell among thorns, which grew up and choked it. Part of it, finally, landed on good soil and yielded grain a hundred or sixty or thirty fold.

In Matthew's interpretation (13:18–23), however, it is turned into an allegory concerning the different trials of the life of faith.

> The seed along the path is the man who hears the message about God's reign without understanding it. The evil one approaches him to steal away what was sown in his mind. The seed that fell on patches of rock is the man who hears the message and at first receives it with joy. But he has no roots, so he lasts only for a time. When some setback or persecution involving the message occurs, he soon falters. What was sown among briers is the man who hears the message, but then worldly anxiety and the lure of money choke it off. Such a one produces no yield. But what was sown on good soil is the man who hears the message and takes it in. He it is who bears a yield of a hundred or sixty or thirty fold.

This interpretation is Matthew's creative adaptation of the story to the needs of his community.

*Living in the Real World*

The fourth discourse (chapter 18) is the advice column in Matthew's gospel. This section is addressed to a community struggling with divisions and questions of authority and lifestyle. We could summarize the advice in five points:

1. Power and authority in the church is not to be modeled on the notion of power in the world. Rather, "whoever makes himself lowly ... is of greatest importance in that heavenly reign" (18:4).
2. Scandalous behavior by members of the church is even worse than such behavior by the pagans because it can lead others astray. The believers are to live holy lives.
3. The Christian community is to be one of reconciling love: Then Peter came up and asked him, "Lord, when my

brother wrongs me, how often must I forgive him? Seven times?" "No," Jesus replied, "not seven times; I say seventy times seven times" (18:21–22).
4. Christians are not to take each other to court over their problems but should be able to solve them among themselves in the spirit of charity.
5. The Christian community must be guided by a life of prayer: "Where two or three are gathered in my name, there am I in their midst" (18:20).

## *The Endtime*

The fifth and final discourse (chapters 24 and 25) has to do with the end of time and the judgment of God. The early church believed that the endtime was near. After the death and resurrection of Jesus, it was commonly believed that he would return to establish the kingdom in its fullness. By the time Matthew was written the delay of the parousia had become something of a problem. The church had to reinterpret the meaning of the endtime and the coming of the kingdom. Matthew uses imagery and language from the book of Daniel to talk about the impending judgment. He uses the title "Son of Man" which is found in Daniel to refer to the messiah as he ushers in the final kingdom. Yet Matthew remains extremely humble about when the end will occur. According to him only the Father knows this (not even the Son): "As for the exact day or hour, no one knows it, neither the angels in heaven nor the Son, but the Father only" (24:36). In the meantime Christians are to lead lives of vigilance, always attentive to the possible coming of the Lord (the parable of the virgins, Matthew 25:1–12). Ultimately, however, judgment will depend on how we have treated our brothers and sisters:

"When the Son of Man comes in his glory, escorted by all the angels of heaven, he will sit upon his royal throne, and all the nations will be assembled before him. Then he will separate them into two groups, as a shepherd separates sheep from goats. The sheep he will place on his right hand, the goats on his left. The king will say to those on his right: 'Come! You have my Father's blessing! Inherit the kingdom prepared for you from the creation of the world. For I was hungry and you gave me food, I was thirsty and you gave me drink. I was a stranger and you welcomed me, naked and you clothed me. I was ill and you comforted me, in prison and you came to visit me.' Then the just will ask him: 'Lord, when did we see you hungry and feed you or see you thirsty and give you drink? When did we welcome you away from home or clothe you in your nakedness? When did we visit you when you were ill or in prison?' The king will answer them: 'I assure you, as often as you did it for one of my least brothers, you did it for me' " (Matthew 25:31–40).

## Luke

### *Love Without Boundaries*

If Matthew is concerned with proving that Jesus is the fulfillment of the Old Testament, **Luke wants to show that Jesus' mission and meaning transcends the Jews and is for all persons.** In fact, Luke seems to have a broader view of salvation history in which the church carries on the mission of Christ into the indefinite future. Luke's gospel is the first part of a two volume series. The second part is the **Acts of the Apostles** which describes the development of the church from its origins in Jerusalem to its foundation in Rome, the great capital of the nations. Luke is intent on showing that Christianity goes beyond Jerusalem and the Jews. It is intended for the whole world. The universality of Luke's perspective can be seen in his genealogy of Jesus. Whereas Matthew traced the genealogy of Jesus to Abraham in order to show that Jesus is the fulfillment of Israel, Luke traces it all the way back to Adam, the father of mankind (see Luke 3:23–38). **For Luke, there are no boundaries to God's saving love.** This means that salvation has come not only for the Jews but for the Gentiles as well, and in a special way for the poor, the oppressed and the outcast. Luke's gospel is sometimes referred to as the gospel of compassion and mercy because these values are stressed so thoroughly throughout.

Luke begins the public ministry of Jesus with an explanation of the type of Messiah that he will be: one who has come for the poor and oppressed. Upon returning to Nazareth, Jesus goes to the synagogue where he reads from the scroll of the prophet Isaiah:

> The spirit of the Lord is upon me;
> therefore he has anointed me.
> He has sent me to bring glad tidings to the poor,
> to proclaim liberty to captives,
> recovery of sight to the blind and release to prisoners,
> to announce a year of favor from the Lord (Luke 4: 16–19).

*Good News: A Time of Mercy*

**Luke took every opportunity to emphasize that the mission of Jesus was one of mercy and reconciliation.** For example, it is only in Luke that we find the famous parable of the prodigal son (Luke 15:11–32) which remains the classic description of the merciful, unconditional love of the Father. This story is better named the parable of the loving father because he is certainly the key figure. The prodigal son is not a very good model of conversion. It is only when he is reduced to feeding pigs that he makes the very pragmatic decision to return home. That is just common sense. It is the behavior of the father that is truly striking. He gives the boy the inheritance long before he has any right to it. And then he runs to greet him (a completely undignified act for a Jewish elder) when he returns home. Both Luke and Jesus portray God as one who rejoices in the love he has for his children. It is this completely unreasonable compassion and exuberant love for sinners that the Pharisees (represented by the older brother in the parable) cannot comprehend.

Likewise, the parable of the good Samaritan (Luke 10:25–36) is found only in Luke also. This is more than a parable about the importance of helping others. The hero of the story is the Samaritan, the most despised enemy of the Jews. Again the message is clear: **no one** lies outside the domain of love and salvation.

It is only in Luke that we see Jesus offering forgiveness to the repentant criminal on the cross or saying, "Father, forgive them; they do not know what they are doing" (Luke 23:34a). Luke even weaves this theme into the call of Peter. In Matthew and Mark, Peter and Andrew simply drop their nets to follow Jesus:

> As he made his way along the Sea of Galilee, he observed Simon and his brother Andrew casting their nets into the sea; they were fishermen. Jesus said to them, "Come after me; I will make you fishers of men." They immediately abandoned their nets and became his followers (Mark 1:16–18).

But in Luke, we find a story about conversion and sinfulness. In this version (Luke 5:1–11), Peter has been out fishing and caught nothing. He allows Jesus to use his boat to talk to the crowds. Then it happens. Jesus tells Peter to cast out his nets again. They are filled to the breaking point. Peter, aware that he is in the presence of an extraordinary man, says, "Leave me, Lord, I am a sinful man." But Jesus will not hear of it: "Do not be afraid. From now on you will be catching men." Those reading Luke's gospel would have known of Peter's great prominence in the church, and Luke makes it clear that even the great Peter recognizes his own sinfulness.

*A Universal Lord and Savior*

**Jesus' virtues of love, forgiveness, compassion for the poor and care for the oppressed make him truly a universal figure,** and this too is not lost on the author of the gospel. Luke's gospel was written in a climate in which the Roman world had become suspicious and even hostile to Christians. Nero's persecution of the Christians in 64 A.D. had set the stage for such an attitude. Luke is, in some ways, trying to reconcile the Christian faith with the Roman world. He dates the birth of Jesus with a decree of the Roman emperor and has the Roman governor Pilate declare that Jesus was innocent. (In the Acts of the Apostles, Paul is often brought before Roman magistrates and acquitted of charges.)

When we read the gospel of Luke we begin to realize more clearly than ever that Jesus' role in salvation history is unique for all time and all people. Luke's vision is "catholic" in the truest sense of the word: universal and all-embracing.

## Summary

1. Mark's gospel focuses on the theme of the messianic secret.
2. In Mark, Jesus is gradually revealed as the messiah but one

who transcends the religious and political expectations of the people.
3. The role of suffering in the life of Jesus plays a very important role in the gospel of Mark.
4. Matthew's gospel puts greater emphasis on the teaching of Jesus.
5. Matthew wishes to show that Jesus is the new Moses who fulfills the law and the prophets.
6. Matthew's gospel revolves around five discourses or teachings of Jesus.
7. Luke's gospel locates Jesus in the context of universal salvation history: beginning with the Jews and finding fulfillment in Jesus and the church.
8. Luke portrays Jesus in very human, merciful and compassionate characteristics that can be appreciated not only by Jews but by any person of good faith.

## Study Questions

1. What is the messianic secret in Mark's gospel?

2. Why does Jesus keep his identity a secret?

3. What is the basis of the argument between Peter and Jesus in Mark 8?

4. What is the basic structure and outline of Mark's gospel?

5. How is Matthew's gospel different from Mark's?

6. What are some ways in which Matthew tries to show that Jesus fulfills the Old Testament?

7. How does Matthew use the Sermon on the Mount to compare Jesus with Moses?

8. How does Matthew adapt the parable of the seed to the needs of his listeners?

9. What is the basic structure of Matthew's gospel?

10. How are the genealogies of Matthew and Luke different? Why are they different?

11. What is one of the main themes in Luke's gospel?

12. Why is the parable of the good Samaritan typical of Luke's concerns?

13. What is meant by Luke's universalism?

# 5

# The Gospel of John

*Author, Date and Audience*

Many people simply assume that the author of John's gospel is the apostle. Scripture scholars today do not believe that. In biblical times, it was common to ascribe authorship to a great person in order to give a work greater authority. There is, however, good reason to believe that much of the gospel was written by one of John's followers and is based on the teaching and preaching of the apostle. The gospel has also gone through a second stage of editing, in which new passages were added (most notably the beginning and the end). So **when we talk about the authorship of John we are really talking about a complex sequence of events that includes preaching, writing and later editing.**

It is commonly accepted that John's gospel is the last of the four to be written probably near the end of the first century A.D. (90–100). It is written to a community that has its own unique problems and questions. They were dealing with the animosity and hostility of the Jewish leaders who had expelled Christians from the synagogues. For this reason, there is something of an anti-Jewish polemic within John's gospel. It should be noted, however, that whenever John uses the term "the Jews" in a negative sense, he is always referring to their leaders and not to the Jews as a people.

**The differences between this gospel and the synoptics are striking.** We have seen how Matthew, Mark and Luke share a great deal of material in common. They certainly have their own special characteristics but, on the whole, their similarities outweigh their differences. John is aware of the synoptic tradition but makes very little use of it. His style, language, theology, structure and sources have given him a unique and celebrated role within the New Testament.

*Language*

It is not necessary to read any further than the first verse to realize that the language in John's gospel is very different from that of the synoptics. John uses language much more symbolically. The opening line: "In the beginning was the word" contains language not found elsewhere in the gospels. Light and darkness, life, sign, glory, flesh and spirit and eternal life are all typical of Johannine language that is filled with figurative meaning.

*Jesus*

John's gospel paints a truly unique portrait of Jesus. It is a view of Jesus seen almost entirely from a heavenly perspective. Jesus is the full revelation of the Father, the pre-existent Son of God. The divine nature of Jesus shines through the human. There is no better example of this than Jesus' attitude toward his death. In the synoptics, the human Jesus is filled with dread and fear and prays for strength from his Father. In John, these human qualities are overcome by the all-knowing Jesus. Compare the two accounts, one from Mark and one from John.

| Mark | John |
|---|---|
| Then he began to be filled with fear and distress. He said to them, "My heart is filled with sorrow to the point of death. Remain here and stay awake." He advanced a little and fell to the ground, praying that if it were possible this hour might pass him by (Mark 14:34–35). | "My soul is troubled now, yet what should I say—Father, save me from this hour? But it was for this that I came to this hour. Father, glorify your name!" (John 12:27–28a). |

**John transforms Jesus' hour of dread into an hour of glory.** The human anxiety involved in facing death has been stripped away. In Mark, Jesus prays that the hour might pass him by. In John, this prayer is considered and dismissed.

Nor is their any hiddenness to the identity of Jesus in John. In the very first chapter, Andrew tells Simon, "We have found the Messiah!" and Nathaniel proclaims to Jesus: "You are the Son of God; you are the king of Israel." Contrast this with the synoptic version where the apostles gradually come to understand Jesus, and never fully understand him until the resurrection. In John, this post-resurrectional faith is often placed on the lips of pre-resurrectional characters.

Jesus himself seems to have an explicit self-knowledge far beyond the synoptic portrayal. He refers to himself as the Son of God and predicts his death and resurrection at the beginning of the public ministry (John 2:18–22). He understands himself not so much as the Jewish messiah promised of old, but in the plan of universal salvation history. He summarizes his role to Nicodemus: "Yes, God so loved the world that he gave his only Son, that whoever believes in him may not die but may have eternal life" (John 3:16). **This understanding of Jesus reflects a highly developed faith that**

**only came to be after his resurrection but is projected back into the life of Christ.**

*The Teaching of Jesus*

John's gospel emphasizes themes that are only implicit in the synoptic gospels. The message of Jesus himself is transformed into a new expression of Christian faith. Two major themes can be discerned in Jesus' teaching in John:

1. *Jesus and the Father are one.* As we have seen, the synoptics present the teaching of Jesus in terms of the coming of the reign of God. In John, this reign, or kingdom, goes virtually unmentioned. Instead **Jesus speaks mostly about himself.** This, however, is not inconsistent with the synoptic message because for John, Jesus is the kingdom of God in the flesh. In the fourth gospel, there are a whole series of I AM sayings in which Jesus reveals himself. Some of these are symbolic descriptions. For example:

"I am the bread of life" (John 7:35).
"I am the light of the world" (John 8:12).
"I am the sheepgate" (John 10:7).
"I am the good shepherd" (John 10:11).
"I am the resurrection and the life" (John 11:25).
"I am the way, the truth and the life" (John 14:6).
"I am the true vine" (John 15:1).

In each of these descriptions, Jesus goes on to make uses of the symbolism, drawn mostly from Jewish and Christian sources, to explain his relationship to the believer and the church. There are a series of I AM sayings, however, that have a deeper Christological meaning. The verb for I AM in Hebrew forms the root of the word "Yahweh," the divine name revealed to Moses. John uses certain I AM passages to identify Jesus with Yahweh:

"You will surely die in your sins unless you come to believe that I AM" (John 8:24).

"When you lift up the Son of Man you will realize that I AM" (John 8:28).

"Before Abraham came to be, I AM" (John 8:58).

"I tell you this now before it takes place, so that when it does take place you may believe that I AM" (John 13:19).

The sense of these passages is unclear unless we realize the theological motive behind them: Jesus identifies himself with Yahweh, God.

2. *Eternal life.* In addition to talking about himself, Jesus also speaks often of "eternal life," and this can be confusing because he does not use it in the same sense that it is used today concerning the immortality of the person. Eternal life, for John, has more to do with a quality of life than a length of life: "Eternal life is this: to know you the only true God and him whom you have sent, Jesus Christ" (John 17:3). In this sense, eternal life has begun in the earthly life of the believer and continues beyond death. From John's perspective, the enemy of eternal life is not death but sin. This is an example of what the Johannine scholars call "**realized eschatology**." Put simply, this means that Christian fulfillment begins on this side of the tomb. This is in contrast to a future eschatology that looks to the next life as the source of God's salvation and human fulfillment (see Matthew 24–25). John's gospel is the strongest of the four in its emphasis on realized eschatology.

## *John's Unique Style*

Jesus' message in John differs not only in content but in style. In the synoptics, Jesus teaches, often using parables and short sayings. In John, **there are instead long, symbolic theological discourses. None of the synoptic parables can be found in John.**

The evangelist also makes great use of double meaning and **irony.** Jesus often says something only to be misunderstood by his listeners because they have missed the figurative meaning. His advice to Nicodemus that a man be "born from above" is met with the response: "How can a man be born again once he is old? ... Can he return to his mother's womb and be born over again?" (John 3:4). He has taken the literal meaning and missed the symbolic one. Jesus is talking about spiritual rebirth. John often uses these misunderstandings as the basis for explaining the true meaning of Jesus' message. Likewise, there are quite a few ironic passages in John in which a true statement about Jesus is unknowingly spoken by an unbeliever. For example, when Jesus promises the Samaritan woman living water, she replies, "Surely you do not pretend to be greater than our ancestor Jacob, who gave us this well" (John 4:12). The reader, of course, knows the ironic answer to that question.

## *Replacement of Jewish Feasts and Religious Ideas*

One of the strong themes in John's gospel has to do with Jesus replacing the Jewish feasts and traditions in the plan of salvation. This theme is even stronger than the synoptic theme of fulfillment. Because of the bitter controversy between Christians and Jews, John wants to make it clear that in Jesus something completely new has taken place. The old has been replaced by the new. Note how consistent this theme is through the first half of the gospel.

**a. The wedding feast of Cana** (John 2:1–11). At his mother's request, Jesus performs the first of his signs. The wedding he is attending has run out of wine. Present were six stone water jars prescribed for Jewish ceremonial washings. Jesus turns the water into wine. When the waiter in charge tastes it he remarks that the choicest wine has been saved for last. The story is filled with symbolism. Jesus has replaced the prescribed Jewish waters with the choicest wine. In the Old Testament, wine is a common symbol for the messianic banquet which Jesus is inaugurating.

**b. The cleansing of the temple** (John 2:13–22). Jesus chases the moneychangers from the temple precincts and vows that those who would "destroy this temple" will see it raised up in three days. He replaces the temple with his own body, his own self which will become the center of faith.

**c. The Samaritan woman** (John 4:4–25). One of the points of contention between Samaritans and Jews was the location of the temple. Jews worshiped in Jerusalem, Samaritans on Mount Gerizim. In this passage Jesus replaces both forms of worship: "Authentic worshipers will worship the Father in spirit and truth" (John 4:23).

**d. The cure on the sabbath feast** (John 5:1–18). Jesus heals a paralytic on the sabbath. The inactivity of the sabbath has been replaced by the "works" of Jesus. To those who objected, Jesus replied, "My Father is at work until now, and I am at work as well" (John 5:17).

**e. The bread of life discourse** (John 6:25–58). John uses this discourse in the context of the Jewish Passover to show that Jesus as the bread of life has replaced the manna of the exodus. "Your ancestors ate manna in the desert but they died. This is the bread that comes down from heaven for a man to eat and never die. I myself am the living bread come down from heaven" (John 6:49–51a).

**f. The feast of Booths (or Tabernacles)** (John 7:1–38). Jesus travels to Jerusalem for the feast of Booths. This feast originated as a fall harvest celebration and included prayers for rain. At the time of Jesus, it was a very important feast and focused on the symbolism of water. On each of the seven days of the feast, water would be drawn from the fountain of Gihon and carried to the temple. "On the last and greatest day of the festival, Jesus stood up and cried out: 'If anyone thirsts, let him come to me; let him drink who believes in me' " (John 7:37). Jesus replaces the waters of this feast with himself, and, implicitly, with the waters of baptism.

**g. The feast of Dedication** (John 10:22–39). Jesus is still in Jerusalem for the feast of Dedication or Chanukah, celebrating the victory of the Maccabees over the Syrians who had desecrated the Jewish temple. The feast of Dedication celebrated the rebuilding of the altar and each year it was rededicated or consecrated. It is in this context that Jesus refers to himself as the one "whom the Father consecrated" (10:36). Once again, Jesus has replaced the Jewish feast with his own person.

*The Prologue: John 1:1–18*

> In the beginning was the Word;
> the Word was in God's presence,
> and the Word was God.
> He was present to God in the beginning.
> Through him all things came into being,
> and apart from him nothing came to be.
> Whatever came to be in him, found life,
> life for the light of men.
> The light shines on in darkness,
> a darkness that did not overcome it.
>
> There was a man named John sent by God, who came as a witness to testify to the light, so that through him all men might believe—but only to testify to the light, for he himself was not the light. The real light which gives light to every man was coming into the world.

He was in the world,
and through him the world was made,
yet the world did not know who he was.
To his own he came,
yet his own did not accept him.
Any who did accept him
he empowered to become children of God.

These are they who believe in his name—who were begotten not by blood, nor by carnal desire, nor by man's willing it, but by God.

The Word became flesh
and made his dwelling among us,
and we have seen his glory:
The glory of an only Son coming from the
  Father,
filled with enduring love.

John testified to him by proclaiming: "This is he of whom I said, 'The one who comes after me ranks ahead of me, for he was before me.'"

Of his fullness
we have all had a share—
love following upon love.

For while the law was given through Moses, this enduring love came through Jesus Christ. No one has ever seen God. It is God the only Son, ever at the Father's side, who has revealed him.

This prologue was originally an early Christian hymn which was adapted to serve as an introduction to the gospel.

In it we find many of the central theological ideas in the gospel.

The prologue begins with the same words that begin the book of Genesis: "In the beginning." Immediately, the reader is being introduced to a highly developed understanding of Jesus. He was "in the beginning." **He is the pre-existent Word of God present from the dawn of creation.** Christians today may take this picture for granted, but at the time it represented a new and creative insight into the person of Jesus. Whereas Mark introduces the divinity of Jesus at his baptism ("This is my Son, the beloved") and Matthew and Luke at his birth (the infancy narratives and the virginal conception), John traces the divine nature of Jesus back to the dawn of time.

John uses "**the Word**" to represent Christ. The expression "the word of the Lord" has a rich tradition in the Old Testament as God's communication to his people through his prophets. Jesus, as the Word, is the communication and self-revelation of the Father. He is the source of all creation and is present to all creation as light in the midst of darkness. Wherever God makes his presence known, the Word takes shape. The hymn explains that the Word was always in the world but the world did not know him. Finally, the climax of this hymn is described in verse 14: "The Word became flesh and made his dwelling among us, and we have seen his glory, the glory of an only Son coming from the Father filled with enduring love." At the heart of this gospel is a theology of the **incarnation:** God has become a human being. The word "glory" that is used to describe the Son is an important one in John's gospel. In the Old Testament it refers to the visible manifestation of the power of the invisible God. In John, the glory of God can be seen in Jesus throughout his public ministry in his "signs" (miracles), but it is his death and resurrection that fully reveal the glory of the Father. As Jesus

## "Who Do People Say That I Am?"

There was not a Jew on earth who believed that the messiah would be God in the flesh. This notion of the incarnation, which we see so strongly in John's gospel, took many years for the early church to develop and discover. Jesus left no theological blueprint on who he was in relationship to the Father. It was left to the church, guided by his Spirit, to reflect on that mystery and to explain it as well as possible. They knew there was only one God and yet they believed that Jesus and the Father were one. When we look at the New Testament, we can detect a steady development of ideas leading to the incarnation. At first, Jesus is described as being made Lord at his resurrection and glorification. Later, the gospel authors want to show that Jesus was also Lord and Savior throughout his ministry (Mark), from his birth (Matthew and Luke), and even from the dawn of creation (John).

**The Acts of the Apostles** reflects the proclamation of the earliest church: "Therefore let the house of Israel know beyond any doubt that God has made both Lord and Messiah this Jesus whom you crucified" (Acts 2:36). It seems that the church originally saw the resurrection as the moment of Jesus' lordship.

**Mark** begins his gospel with the baptism of Jesus which is the beginning of his public ministry. For Mark, it is here that Jesus' role as the messiah begins: "Immediately upon coming up out of the water he saw the sky rent in two and the Spirit descending on him like a dove. Then a voice came from the heavens: 'You are my beloved son. On you my favor rests'" (Mark 1:1–11).

**Matthew and Luke** take the lordship of Jesus back to its next logical step. From the moment of his conception and birth, Jesus is the messiah come into the world: "Joseph, son of David, have no fear about taking Mary for your wife. It is by the Holy Spirit that she has conceived this child. She is to have a son and you are to name him Jesus because he will save his people from their sins" (Matthew 1:20b–21).

**John** proclaims that Jesus is the pre-existent Word of God made flesh. He was always in union with God from the beginning of time: "In the beginning was the Word; the Word was in God's presence, and the Word was God" (John 1:1).

The development that took place was one that moved from an emphasis on what Jesus did (died and rose) to who Jesus is in the depth of his being (the eternal Son of God).

is facing his death, he prays: "Father, the hour has come! Give glory to your Son that your Son may give glory to you... a glory I had with you before the world began" (John 17:1,5b).

In the midst of this hymn, the gospel editor injects two passages concerning John the Baptist. They seem somewhat out of place but have a very practical purpose. Both of the passages emphasize the superiority of Jesus over the Baptist and the fact that the Baptist is not the messiah. Scholars believe that this was done to combat a group who still were following the Baptist and awaiting the messiah. These passages make it clear that the role of the Baptist was to point to Jesus: "He (John) came as a witness to testify for the light... but only to testify to the light, for he himself was not the light" (John 1:7–8).

*The Book of Signs (John 1:19–12:50)*

The next major division within John's gospel is the book of signs. This section of the gospel contains the public ministry of Jesus in which he reveals himself as the revelation of the Father through his words and "signs." These signs are miracles. In many ways, they are similar to the synoptic miracle stories. (In fact, three of them can be found in the synoptics.) The major difference comes about in their function in the gospel. As we have already seen, the miracles in the synoptics signify the power of the reign of God breaking into history. In John, there is no theme concerning God's reign. The signs have a largely symbolic and Christological meaning. Like most of this gospel, they point beyond themselves to Jesus. There are seven signs in John which reveal the glory of Jesus. (The number seven symbolizes fullness and perfection.) Here we will briefly list the sign and the key meaning behind it:

**1. The wedding feast of Cana** (John 2:1–11). We

have already seen that this miracle symbolizes Jesus' ushering in the new messianic era (symbolized by the abundance of wine and the banquet) and his replacement of the former Jewish traditions.

**2. The healing of the royal official's son** (John 4:46–54). The key to this story is that the miracle occurs for a pagan and his whole household is converted. This symbolizes the fact that Jesus has come for Gentiles as well as Jews. He is the Savior of all mankind.

**3. The cure on the sabbath feast** (John 5:1–15). This sign points to Jesus' power over the sabbath. This theme can also be found in the synoptics (e.g. Mark 3:1–6). However, John wants to show that the source of Jesus' power over the sabbath is his union with the Father. His rebuttal to the accusations of the Pharisees in this matter reveal the meaning of the miracle: "I solemnly assure you, the Son cannot do anything by himself—he can only do what he sees the Father doing. For whatever the Father does the Son does likewise" (John 5:19).

**4. Multiplication of the loaves** (John 6:1–13). This miracle is linked with the bread of life discourse and reveals Jesus as the fulfillment of the exodus, replacing the manna with his own body and blood. This miracle in particular has strong eucharistic overtones. In the Eucharist, the one body of Christ is miraculously given to thousands (today, millions).

**5. Jesus walks on water** (John 6:16–21). This miracle seems to bring together a number of different traditions about Jesus walking on water. For John, the key to this sign may lie in the words of Jesus: "It is I," literally I AM. As we have seen, this may be John's way of identifying Jesus with God.

**6. The cure of the man born blind** (John 9:1–7). This miracle echoes some of the symbolism found in the prologue. Jesus is the light that has come into the world. In

John, light is a symbol for truth and darkness a symbol for sin or confusion. This miracle points beyond the physical darkness of blindness to the spiritual darkness of sin. The story is followed by a conflict with the Jewish leaders who represent the spiritual darkness and their unwillingness to accept Jesus as the light.

**7. The raising of Lazarus from the dead** (John 11:1–44). The key to this sign is in its timing. Jesus is on his way to Jerusalem where he will be put to death. The death and rising of Lazarus is meant as a prefiguring of the death and resurrection of Jesus. Likewise, faith in Jesus allows the believer to share in his death and resurrection. Again, the point of the miracle is to teach us about Jesus: "I am the resurrection and the life" (John 11:25).

*The Book of Glory (John 13:1–20:31)*

This section of John's gospel reveals the glory of Jesus in his death, resurrection and ascension. It includes the story of the Last Supper, the last discourse, the arrest and trial of Jesus, and his death and resurrection. Since a different chapter of this book is devoted to the death and resurrection of Jesus, we will focus here on the Last Supper and the Last Discourse.

*The Last Supper in John*

By the time this gospel was written, the Eucharist had been celebrated by Christians for over fifty years. The synoptics tell the story of the final meal of Jesus and his apostles that became the basis for the Eucharist. John, however, leaves out the details of the meal. In fact, his readers would have been familiar with those events already. Instead, he portrays the Last Supper in highly symbolic terms with a story of Jesus washing the feet of the apostles. John's theology of the Eucharist is best understood in chapter 6 in the bread of life discourse.

In John, on the night before his death, at the meal he celebrated with his apostles, Jesus rose and washed their feet. This custom was part of Palestinian hospitality. When a guest would arrive, the servant of the host would wash his feet which would have been dusty from the walk. Jesus, thus, takes on the role of the servant. Obviously, the meaning of the act was symbolic and John explains it:

> After he had washed their feet, he put his cloak back on and reclined at table once more. He said to them: "Do you understand what I just did for you? You address me as 'Teacher' and 'Lord,' and fittingly enough, for that is what I am. But if I washed your feet—I who am Teacher and Lord—then you must wash each other's feet. What I just did was to give you an example: as I have done, so you must do" (John 13:12–15).

There are several layers of meaning to this story: First, by connecting it to the Last Supper, John has implicitly tied the meaning of the story to the Eucharist. The Christian community is not only to celebrate the Eucharist—they are to live it. The ritual without the service to each other is empty. Second, the washing of the feet has baptismal symbolism as well. Baptism is a sharing in the death and resurrection of Jesus. By situating this story right before the passion, death and resurrection, John is also teaching about baptism. That is why Jesus says to Peter, "If I do not wash you, you will have no share in my heritage." Baptism unites us with Christ. Finally, this story has meaning on the level of ministry in the church. Leadership in the church is not power in the normal understanding of the word. Christian power lies in service and in humility as exemplified by Jesus.

This story fits as the perfect lead-in to the book of glory.

For as we shall see, Jesus' glory lies in his love unto death. This story symbolizes exactly that.

## *The Last Discourse*

Chapters 14 through 17 comprise the last discourse in John's gospel. These four chapters are fashioned in the style of a farewell address from Jesus to the disciples in the context of the Last Supper. Farewell addresses are very common in the Old Testament and can be associated with Abraham, Joshua, David and Moses. In fact, the entire book of Deuteronomy is composed of Moses' farewell addresses to the people of Israel. These four chapters in John represent for many the height of New Testament spirituality. They have consistently been the favorites of the great spiritual writers and mystics because of their constant return to the theme of unity between the Father and the Son and those who believe in the Son.

## *The Vine and the Branches*

On the unity between the Father and Son, Jesus is at his most explicit in these chapters: "Whoever has seen me has seen the Father.... Do you not believe that I am in the Father and the Father is in me?" (John 14: 9,10a). Likewise those who believe in Jesus will be united with him and the Father. The sign of the true believer is love. John develops this theme through the image of the vine and the branches (John 15:1–17):

> I am the true vine and my Father is the vine-grower.... No more than a branch can bear fruit of itself apart from the vine, can you bear fruit apart from me.... He who lives in me and I in him will produce abundantly (John 15:1,4,5a).

The image of the vine to represent Israel is a common one used by the prophets in the Old Testament (cf. Hosea 10:1, Jeremiah 6:9; Ezekiel 15:1–6). In the vineyard song of Isaiah 5:1–7, Yahweh laments that he has planted the choicest of vines only to have it yield wild grapes. However, in John the vine no longer is Israel. Jesus is the *true* vine. Here again we see the theme of replacement in John. Jesus has replaced Israel as God's means of salvation. In the allegory, the Father is the vinegrower just as he is in Isaiah.

What is the connective between Father, Son and disciple? John answers it this way: "As the Father has loved me, so I have loved you. Live on in my love" (John 15:9).

## *The Paraclete*

Jesus also seeks to assure his disciples that his death will not mean the end of his presence to them:

> I will ask the Father and he will give you another Paraclete—to be with you always; the Spirit of truth, whom the world cannot accept, since it neither sees him nor recognizes him; but you can recognize him because he remains with you and will be within you.

The term that Jesus uses for the Spirit, "Paraclete," is a legal one meaning an advocate or spokesman. The Spirit is God's spokesman. He is "another" Paraclete because Jesus is the first. The Spirit becomes the operating principle of faith after the death and resurrection of Jesus. Those who live in Christ have his Spirit, and the Spirit continues to guide and lead the church: "I have much more to tell you, but you cannot bear it now. When he comes, however, being the Spirit of truth he will guide you to all truth" (John 16:12,13a).

*Jesus Prays for the Apostles*

Often in the farewell addresses of the Old Testament, the speaker would end with a prayer for the people he is to leave behind. This is precisely what we find at the end of the last discourse. Jesus prays for his disciples. There are two key elements to his prayer: first, they are to be protected by God's name which he has given them; and, second, they are to be consecrated in truth. In the Hebrew mentality, the name denotes the whole person and the meaning of that person. Thus, Christians pray in the Lord's Prayer, "Hallowed be thy name." That means a lot more than not saying "God damn it." It means that God will be the number one priority in my life. Thus to be protected by God's name means to be protected from the power of sin by giving God authority in one's life. When Jesus prays that the apostles be consecrated in truth, they are to be holy because they will be God's representatives and God is holy. Being consecrated in the truth means being consecrated in God's word ("Your word is truth"—17:7) and thus it means being consecrated in Jesus who is God's Word.

## Summary

1. John's gospel was the last of the four written, and much of it is based on unique sources unlike those in the synoptic tradition.
2. Much of the language in John's gospel is symbolic.
3. John's portrait of Jesus is that of the pre-existent Son of God who reveals the Father.
4. Many of the claims made about Jesus (by the apostles and Jesus) reflect a post-resurrectional understanding of Jesus' divinity.

5. Jesus does not speak about the reign of God, but speaks mostly about himself and eternal life.
6. None of the narrative parables of the synoptics are in John.
7. One of the main themes of John's gospel is replacement. Jesus replaces the feasts and traditions of Israel.
8. The prologue is an early Christian hymn that is used as an introduction to the gospel and describes Jesus as the Word made flesh.
9. The book of signs contains the public ministry of Jesus in which he reveals himself through his highly symbolic miracles ("signs").
10. The book of glory is the revelation of the glory of Jesus through his death and resurrection. It also contains the last discourse which is Jesus' farewell address to the apostles.

## Study Questions

1. How is John's gospel different from those of the synoptics?

2. What is the main idea concerning Jesus that John wishes to communicate?

3. What is meant by a post-resurrectional view of Jesus?

4. How is the teaching of Jesus in John different from that in the synoptics?

5. Give five examples of the theme of replacement in the gospel of John.

6. Why does this gospel begin with the words, "In the beginning"?

7. Why does John refer to Jesus as the Word?

8. What is meant by the incarnation? What line in the prologue refers to the incarnation?

9. What is a sign? What is the purpose of a sign in John's gospel? Give an example.

10. Why is the word "glory" important when associated with Jesus?

11. What is the ultimate hour of Jesus' glory?

12. Explain the symbolism of the story of the washing of the feet.

13. What is the meaning of the allegory of the vine and the branches?

14. Who is the Paraclete? What is his role?

# 6

# The Death and Resurrection of Jesus

What comes at the end of this book actually comes first in the Christian proclamation of faith. As Paul wrote to the church in Corinth: "I handed on to you what I myself received, that Christ died for our sins in accordance with the Scriptures; that he was buried and, in accordance with the Scriptures, rose on the third day." The letters of Paul in the New Testament, which were written before the gospels, revolve around the death and resurrection of Jesus as the center of Christian faith. There is virtually no mention of the deeds or miracles of Jesus, nor an attempt to explain his teaching. **Biblical scholars attest that the earliest stories to be formulated in the oral tradition were the stories of Jesus' death.** His death was important not because Jesus was a martyr for a cause but because his death summed up his entire life and, in itself, had extraordinary theological significance. The understanding and meaning of Jesus' death became core to Christian faith. As Paul says above, "Christ died **for our sins.**" His death is seen as the great act of salvation. Everything else in the gospels presupposes this. There is no way to understand the gospels or Christianity without understanding the death and resurrection of Jesus.

## Prelude: The Message of Jesus

The idea that the messiah would suffer and die was not in the consciousness of the people at the time of Christ. We have already seen how the political and nationalistic expectations of the people were rejected by Jesus. But his perception of his mission was never really understood by anyone else. In fact, Jesus' death was the culmination of his message that taught, "Whoever would preserve his life will lose it, but whoever loses his life for my sake and the gospel's will preserve it" (Mark 8:35). In the synoptics we see that Jesus predicts his fate three times (e.g. see Mark 8:31; 9:31; 10:33–34), but his message was unacceptable to his followers. Peter begins to argue with him (Mark 8:32); or they fail to understand him (Mark 9:32); or James and John ask Jesus for a share in his power and glory (Mark 10:35–37). Jesus' message of self-surrender seems completely lost on them.

## Entry into Jerusalem

John and the synoptics differ on the number of times that Jesus visits Jerusalem. John reports several visits while the synoptics mention only one. Most scholars today prefer the Johannine chronology as it would better explain the pervasiveness of Jesus' opposition. Regardless, each of the four gospels agree that **Jesus' final trip to Jerusalem is occasioned by the feast of the Passover.** The city would have been teeming with Jewish pilgrims from throughout Palestine and the surrounding countries. Likewise all four agree that Jesus' entry into Jerusalem is a triumphant one:

> They brought the colt to Jesus and threw their cloaks across its back, and he sat on it. Many people spread their cloaks on the road, while others spread reeds which they had cut in the fields. Those preced-

ing him as well as those who followed cried out: "Hosanna! Blessed is he who comes in the name of the Lord! Blessed is the reign of our father David to come! Hosanna in the highest!" (Mark 11:7–10).

The image of Jesus riding on the donkey mirrors Zechariah 9:9 in the Old Testament: "Rejoice heartily, O daughter Zion, shout for joy, O daughter Jerusalem! See your king shall come to you; a just savior is he, meek and riding on an ass." It is done by Jesus to help counteract the nationalistic expectations of the messiah. The passage in Zechariah speaks of a different type of messiah who is meek and will bring peace to the nations not just to Israel.

*The Last Supper*

All three synoptic gospels include the story of the Last Supper with some small variations in their accounts. As we have seen, John does not include the story of the meal itself although he does mention the occasion and connects it to the story of the washing of the feet. The synoptics portray the meal as **seder** or Passover meal, and in order to understand the meaning of the meal, it is necessary to understand its relationship to the Passover.

For the Jewish people, the exodus from Egypt represented the heart of their faith in a God who was present among them as a liberating savior. It was at the exodus that Moses led the Hebrews from their captivity in Egypt into a covenant relationship with Yahweh. It was because of the exodus that the Hebrew people formed their identity as a people in relationship to God. Their journey through the desert to the promised land represented the hopes and aspirations of Jews for all time. It was on Mount Sinai that Moses was given the law by God and had bonded himself to these people:

> Moses went up the mountain to God. Then the Lord called to him and said: "Thus shall you say to the house of Jacob; tell the Israelites: You have seen for yourselves how I treated the Egyptians and how I bore you up on eagle's wings and brought you here to myself. Therefore, if you hearken to my voice and keep my covenant, you shall be my special possession, dearer to me than all other people, though all the earth is mine. You shall be to me a kingdom of priests, a holy nation (Exodus 19:3–6).

Because of the centrality of this event, the Passover was celebrated each year to recall how God had led the Jews from slavery and had entered into a covenant with them. For the Jews, however, the meal did more than recall a past event. It was to make the event present again each year. They were to dress as a people in flight. A lamb was to be roasted to recall the blood of the lamb smeared on the doorposts for their salvation. Only unleavened bread could be eaten to recall the haste with which they traveled. Bitter herbs were eaten to recall the bitterness of the desert. Three glasses of wine were drunk in memory of the covenant. Psalms were sung and the head of the household would repeat the story of the exodus. In the seder meal, they would enact the great event of their history.

It is in the context of this meal that Jesus celebrates the Last Supper with his apostles. But in the course of the meal, he changes its meaning. This is Luke's version of the event:

> When the hour arrived, he took his place at table, and the apostles with him. He said to them: "I have

greatly desired to eat this Passover with you before I suffer. I tell you I will not eat again until it is fulfilled in the kingdom of God."

Then taking a cup he offered a blessing in thanks and said: "Take this and divide it among you; I tell you, from now on I will not drink of the fruit of the vine until the coming of the reign of God."

Then taking bread and giving thanks, he broke it and gave it to them, saying: "This is my body to be given for you. Do this as a remembrance of me." He did the same with the cup after eating, saying as he did so: "This cup is the new covenant in my blood, which will be shed for you."

*Jesus Changes the Meaning of the Meal*

Jesus connects its meaning to his impending death. It is the last time he will eat with his apostles. It is a foreshadowing of the final eschatological banquet associated with the kingdom of God.

He also changes the meaning of the bread. It is no longer the bread of affliction, a reminder of the flight from Egypt. Instead, "This is my body." It is Jesus' body broken for his apostles. It is his very self offered for them ultimately in death.

The meal is now to be celebrated "in remembrance of me." The entire meaning of the meal is being changed and with it the meaning of salvation history. The great act of salvation is no longer the exodus but Jesus himself. The meal is to be celebrated in memory of him.

The cup of wine no longer recalls the old covenant but the new covenant established in Christ and through his death. This language recalls the prophecy of Jeremiah: "The days are coming, says the Lord, when I will make a new covenant with the house of Israel and the house of Judah.... I will place my law within them and write it on their hearts" (Jeremiah 31:31,33b).

Finally, it is no longer the blood of the lamb that brings salvation, but the blood of Jesus.

## *The Arrest and Trial of Jesus*

The four gospels vary somewhat in their details concerning the arrest and trial of Jesus. For our purposes, we will use Mark's version as a guide since it is the earliest of the four accounts.

Jesus is in Gethsemane praying when he is arrested. The scene in the garden has been dramatized somewhat by the evangelists to portray Jesus' fidelity to the Father. If the apostles were in fact asleep, it would be impossible to know what Jesus said in his prayer to the Father. But the words reflect the attitude of Jesus found in the Lord's Prayer: "Father, thy will be done."

Jesus' arrest takes place in the middle of the night because of the Jewish and Roman concern not to excite the masses of people in Jerusalem for the feast. He is brought to the Sanhedrin for a special meeting or trial which was run by the high priest Caiaphas. He is found guilty of blasphemy for claiming to be the messiah, the Son of God. The Sanhedrin condemns him to death but because they did not have the power of capital punishment, Jesus is brought to Pilate and is silent in front of him. Pilate finds no real crime against him, but his ploy of releasing a prisoner for the feast backfires as the people demand Jesus' death.

Underneath this bare bones account lies the question of who is really responsible for Jesus' death: the Jewish leaders or Pilate? Why was Jesus' death necessary? It is difficult to answer this with any certainty but there are some points that may lead us in the right direction.

The chief priests would be threatened by Jesus' presence in Jerusalem. His authority would place theirs in question, and his threat to destroy the temple could have been interpreted as a revolutionary gesture. They must have been concerned with this threat because the evidence brought against Jesus revolves around it (cf. Mark 14:57–58).

In addition, Pilate may not have been the innocent victim that he appears to be. The gospel writers must survive in a Roman world. It is to their benefit to absolve Pilate as much as possible from responsibility. In fact, Pilate seems to become progressively more innocent in the gospels. In Matthew, Pilate washes his hands of the guilt, and in Luke he proclaims Jesus to be innocent three times, even though Pilate's reputation in history is bloodthirsty and anti-Semitic.

Finally, Caiaphas and Pilate held office together for ten years, and it is reasonable to assume that they had learned how to work together or neither would have lasted so long.

**In light of these facts, Jesus' death was most likely a cooperative venture between the Jews and the Romans.** The version that we have in the synoptics has been highly influenced by an anti-Jewish polemic as well as a need to prove to Rome that Christianity was no threat to them.

*The Crucifixion*

Jesus' death by crucifixion is one of the most historically certain facts of his life. This Roman form of execution was reserved for foreigners because of its brutality (Roman citizens were beheaded). All four gospels assert that Jesus is beaten and abused by the soldiers before the crucifixion itself (although in Luke the soldiers are part of Herod's guard, not the Romans'). The abuse revolves around the charge leveled

The early church interpreted the death and resurrection of Jesus in light of Old Testament themes. Psalm 22 and the songs of the suffering servant of Isaiah served as the source of much of the interpretation of the meaning of Jesus' death.

### Psalm 22, verses 1–12

My God, my God, why have you forsaken me,
> far from my prayer, from the words of my cry?

O my God, I cry out by day, and you answer not;
> by night and there is no relief for me.

Yet you are enthroned in the Holy Place,
> O glory of Israel!

In you our fathers trusted; they trusted
> and you delivered them.

To you they cried, and they escaped;
> in you they trusted, and they were not put to shame.

But I am a worm, not a man;
> the scorn of men despised by the people.

All who see me scoff at me;
> they mock me with parted lips, they wag their heads.

"He relied on the Lord; let him deliver him,
> let him rescue him if he loves him."

You have been my guide since I was first formed,
> my security at my mother's breast.

To you I was committed at birth,
> from my mother's womb you are my God.

Be not far from me, for I am in distress;
> be near, for I have no one to help me.

### The Servant of the Lord (Isaiah 53: 3–6)

He was spurned and avoided by men, a man of
 suffering,
 accustomed to infirmity,
One of those from whom men hide their faces,
 spurned
 and we held him in no esteem.

Yet it was our infirmities that he bore,
 our sufferings that he endured,
While we thought of him as striken,
 as one smitten by God and afflicted.
But he was pierced for our offenses
 crushed for our sins;
Upon him was the chastisement that makes us
 whole,
 by his stripes we were healed.
We had all gone astray like sheep.
 each following his own way;
But the Lord laid upon him the guilt of us all.

against him as "king of the Jews." He is given a crown of thorns and a "royal" cloak.

The crucifixion takes place outside the city at a site called Golgotha (the skull place). The prisoner would be forced to carry the crossbar, but because of Jesus' weakened condition a man named Simon the Cyrene is forced to help him. The description of the crucifixion is an extremely simple one in the synoptics without the gory details that have become part of tradition and legend. There were a variety of forms of Roman crucifixion, one of which included nails through the wrists and ankles. Only John's gospel mentions the use of nails. The victims usually died of suffocation, collapsing under the weight of their own bodies. This procedure was sometimes hastened by breaking the legs of the prisoner or by thrusting a lance in his side, neither of which was necessary for Jesus.

The clothing of the condemned man would be shared by the Roman soldiers and in the gospels they are portrayed as casting lots for them. As well as being historically believable, this action also reflects the line from Psalm 22:19: "They divide my garments among them, and for my vesture they cast lots." In fact, Psalm 22 is quoted later in the Passion narrative, this time by Jesus on the cross: "My God, my God, why have you forsaken me?" This raises the question of how much the retelling of the passion and death of Jesus was influenced by the Old Testament.

## *The Resurrection*

As we have mentioned, during his lifetime Jesus was usually misunderstood. This even applies to his own followers. It is only at the resurrection that the meaning of Jesus' words, deeds and death come to light. The resurrection of Jesus becomes the central proclamation of the early church. Yet the meaning of that resurrection is often misunderstood by the contemporary world. We need to return to the New Testament evidence to comprehend the resurrection of Jesus.

What happened? This is the first question that needs to be addressed. Unfortunately, there are no eyewitnesses to the actual event of Jesus' rising from the dead. The gospel witness begins with a story of an empty tomb discovered by the women who came to anoint the body. Thus, despite the artistic portrayals of Jesus emerging from the tomb, there are no claims to witnesses of the resurrection in the New Testament.

Although none claim to have seen the actual resurrection, Christian faith is based on the witness of those who claim that they have met the risen Lord. The gospels contain stories of Jesus' appearances that help reveal the meaning of the event. We will examine five conclusions that can be drawn from these stories:

**1. The resurrection of Jesus is a transformation, not a resuscitation.** The risen Jesus has been radically transformed, not simply brought back to his former existence. There is a very important distinction. In our time, there have been people who have claimed to have been clinically dead only to come back to life again. This is resuscitation. They have returned to the same life with all its limitations. Sooner or later these people will have to die again. The same could be said for the stories in the gospels where Jesus raises someone from the dead (e.g. Lazarus, John 11). Lazarus has come back to life, but he will have to die again.

Jesus, on the other hand, has overcome death. His transformation takes him beyond the limits of time and space. This is apparent in many of the resurrection accounts. When Jesus walks with the disciples on the road to Emmaus (Luke 24:13–25), they fail to recognize him and then he vanishes from their sight. When the apostles were gathered in fear with the door locked, Jesus suddenly appears in their midst (John 20:19–20). Jesus is no longer subject to the same earthly limitations that he had before his death.

**2. The risen Lord is really Jesus.** The gospel accounts go out of their way to emphasize that the resurrection of Jesus was not simply the spiritual resurrection of Jesus that took place in the hearts of his followers. Some would say that Jesus lived on only in spirit. The gospels clearly reject this interpretation. No matter what the nature of Jesus' transformation, it was really Jesus that rose from the dead. Luke attacks this misinterpretation directly:

> While they were still speaking about all of this, he himself stood in their midst. In their panic and fright they thought they were seeing a ghost. He said to them, "Why are you disturbed? Why do such ideas cross your mind? Look at my hands and my feet; It is really I. Touch me and see that a ghost does not have flesh and bones as I do" (Luke 24:36–39).

The gospel accounts are trying to capture and picture an experience that is absolutely unique. It is really Jesus that has risen. The resurrection is a "bodily" one. All of Jesus has been raised. Yet this body has been transformed and is, in many ways, unlike the earthly body. Paul ran into the same problem in the early church when trying to explain the nature of the resurrection to the Christians in Corinth. He tries to compare it to the seed and fruit of a plant: "The seed you sow does not germinate unless it dies. When you sow, you do not sow the full-blown plant but a kernel of wheat or some other grain. God gives body to it as he pleases" (1 Corinthians 15:36–37). No matter what else is said about transformation, Paul and the evangelists also make a great case for continuity between the earthly Jesus and the risen Lord.

**3. The appearances of the risen Lord are experiences of revelation and faith.** One may ask why the risen Lord didn't appear to the members of the Sanhedrin who convicted him or Pilate who sentenced him or the people who rejected him. Finally, now they would believe. They would see the error of their judgments. Yet this does not occur. Perhaps the best explanation is that to meet the risen Lord requires faith. Those who see the risen Lord actually have the risen Lord revealed to them. In some ways this is different than the simple fact of vision. To see the risen Lord is to realize the significance and meaning of the risen Lord. When Mary Magdalene first encounters Jesus she fails to recognize him (John 20:1–18) until he calls her by name. Those who see the Lord are called by the Lord personally. Even Paul, who persecuted the church before meeting the risen Lord, must go through a powerful, wrenching experience of conversion before devoting his life to the service of Christ.

**4. The resurrection is the interpretive key to Jesus and all salvation history.** Before the resurrection, the disciples of Jesus followed him but were unaware of the depth of Jesus' meaning. It is only after the resurrection that Jesus is proclaimed as Lord. It is the resurrection of Jesus that opens the doors of faith to understanding the meaning of both the message and the man. After the resurrection, Jesus the proclaimer of the kingdom becomes the one who is proclaimed. "Doubting" Thomas speaks for all believers when he finally sees the risen Jesus: "My Lord and my God." It is only after the resurrection that the church begins to realize that Jesus is Emmanuel, God among us. Eventually, the church's theology will develop to the point where they recognize that God the

Son has taken flesh in Jesus. Likewise, the church will see in Jesus' resurrection the hope and future of all mankind. Christ's resurrection reveals not only his divinity but the fullness of our humanity. Paul makes the point clearly that it is the humanity of Jesus that offers us our hope: "Christ is now raised from the dead, the first fruits of those who have fallen asleep. Death came through a man, hence the resurrection of the dead comes through a man also. Just as in Adam all die, so in Christ all will come to life again" (1 Corinthians 15:20–22).

**5. The power of Jesus' death and resurrection is available to those who follow him.** Christians often make the mistake of viewing the resurrection only in terms of "proving" that Jesus is God. In fact, the resurrection is also God's offer of salvation to us. We are not only saved from our sins but called into a whole new way of life in which the risen Lord lives in us. When Matthew's gospel ends with Jesus ordering the apostles to make disciples of all nations and to baptize them, we see the risen Lord living on in those who believe in him. Being baptized in the name of the Father and of the Son and of the Holy Spirit is not simply becoming a member of a new religion. It means that Jesus' resurrection will transform our lives. Paul makes this very clear: "Are you not aware that we who were baptized into Christ Jesus were baptized into his death? . . . So that, just as Christ was raised from the dead by the glory of the Father, we too might live a new life" (Romans 6:3–4). The resurrection of Jesus has created a new community of faith and offered us a new way to live in hope.

## Summary

1. Jesus' death and resurrection are at the center of Christian faith and were the main content of the preaching of the early church.

2. Jesus' death is the culmination of his life and message: a life lived in love for others and in total trust of the Father.
3. Jesus' final meal with his apostles symbolizes his impending death and fulfills the Passover ritual.
4. Jesus' death was a collaborative effort between the Romans and the Jews.
5. The crucifixion and death of Jesus is depicted in light of Psalm 22 and Isaiah 53.
6. The resurrection is a transformation (not resuscitation) of Jesus. Yet it is really Jesus that rises from the dead.
7. Meeting the risen Lord was an experience of revelation and faith.
8. It is only after the resurrection that the church realizes the true meaning of Jesus' life and Jesus' unity with the Father.
9. The power of Jesus' resurrection lives on in the community of faith.

## Study Questions

1. What was the significance of Jesus' entry into Jerusalem on the donkey?

2. Why was Jesus in Jerusalem?

3. What was the exodus and how do the Jewish people celebrate it each year?

4. How does Jesus change the meaning of the seder meal?

5. Who was responsible for Jesus' death? Why would the Jewish leaders want him dead? Why would Pilate want him dead?

6. Read Psalm 22 and Isaiah 53. How are these passages reflected in the passion and death of Jesus?

7. The story of the resurrection begins with a discov-

ery of an empty tomb. Why is this an important part of the narrative?

8. What is the difference between resurrection and resuscitation? What are some indications of Jesus' transformation in the gospels?

9. How do the evangelists emphasize that the resurrection of Jesus was a bodily one?

10. In what way is the resurrection of Jesus a present reality as well as a past event?

# Suggested Reading for Further Study and Reflection

## Reference Works

*Jerome Biblical Commentary,* eds. R.E. Brown, J.A. Fitzmyer, R. Murphy. Englewood Cliffs, N.J.: Prentice-Hall, 1968. A comprehensive study of each book in the Bible by Catholic scholars. Includes related articles and maps.

*Harper's Bible Dictionary,* ed. P. Achtemeier. San Francisco: Harper and Row, 1985. Articles by leading scholars on all things biblical.

## Introductions

Harrington, D. *Interpreting the New Testament.* Wilmington: Michael Glazier, 1979/Dublin:Veritas, 1980.

Perkins, P. *Reading the New Testament: An Introduction.* Mahwah, N.J.: Paulist Press, 1978.

Two exceptionally fine and readable works.

## The Gospels in Depth

Best, E. *Mark, the Gospel as Story.* Edinburgh: T. & T. Clark, 1983.

Meier, J.P. *The Vision of Matthew. Christ, Church and Morality in the First Gospel.* Mahwah: Paulist Press, 1978.

LaVerdiere, E. *Luke.* Wilmington: Michael Glazier, 1980.

Brown, R.E. *The Gospel According to John I–XII,* Anchor Bible 29. Garden City: Doubleday, 1966.

Brown, R.E. *The Gospel According to John XIII–XXI,* Anchor Bible 29a. Garden City: Doubleday, 1970.

Brown's books are extraordinary reference works in great depth.

## The Message of the Gospel Today

Greeley, Andrew. *The Jesus Myth. New Insights into the Person and Message of Jesus.* Garden City: Doubleday/Image. 1973.

Shea, John. *The Challenge of Jesus.* Garden City: Doubleday/Image, 1977.